natural wooden toys

75 easy-to-make and kid-safe designs to inspire imaginations & creative play

Erin Freuchtel-Dearing

FOX CHAPEL
PUBLISHING

A Word About Toy Safety

Please use your best parental wisdom when deciding which toys are safe for your child. If you have concerns about your child choking on a small toy, remember that all the toys in this book can be enlarged to whatever size you like. Also keep in mind that toys with parts such as wheels and axles could come apart if not constructed properly and attached with plenty of glue. If you are worried about this, remember that any wheels and axles can be omitted as you create the toys. Use your best judgment and knowledge of your child's behaviors to make the safest choices for your family.

© 2011 by Erin Freuchtel-Dearing and Fox Chapel Publishing Company, Inc., East Petersburg, PA.

Natural Wooden Toys is an original work, first published in 2011 by Fox Chapel Publishing Company, Inc. The patterns contained herein are copyrighted by the author. Readers may make copies of these patterns for personal use. The patterns themselves, however, are not to be duplicated for resale or distribution under any circumstances. Any such copying is a violation of copyright law.

Patterns designed by Nick Dearing.

Thanks to the Art & Creative Materials Institute for allowing the use of their AP seal on page 42.

Thanks to John Kelsey for allowing use of photos from his book, Kid Crafts Woodworking, on pages 22, 30-31.

Published and distributed in North America by Fox Chapel Publishing Company, Inc., East Petersburg, PA.

ISBN 978-1-56523-524-3

Library of Congress Cataloging-in-Publication Data

Freuchtel-Dearing, Erin.

 Natural wooden toys / Erin Freuchtel-Dearing. -- 1st ed.

   p. cm.

 Includes index.

 ISBN 978-1-56523-524-3

 1. Wooden toy making. I. Title.

 TT174.5.W6F674 2011

 745.592--dc22

                    2011008552

To learn more about the other great books from Fox Chapel Publishing, or to find a retailer near you, call toll-free 800-457-9112 or visit us at *www.FoxChapelPublishing.com*.

Note to Authors: We are always looking for talented authors to write new books in our area of woodworking, design, and related crafts. Please send a brief letter describing your idea to Acquisition Editor, 1970 Broad Street, East Petersburg, PA 17520.

Printed in China
First printing: October 2011

acknowledgments

To Kerri, my amazing editor, whose patience and knowledge made the road to becoming an author a wonderful experience. I would also like to thank all the other creative minds at Fox Chapel for their enthusiasm for this project.

To my dear friends and family, thank you for cheering me on and being such great listeners.

To my parents, Barbara and Marc, thank you for believing in me and always encouraging my creativity. Also Mom, thank you for teaching me to sew. I bet you never foresaw where that skill would take me.

To the source of my inspiration and joy—my children, Stella and Elliot. Without their boundless creativity and curiosity, I might have never found my love of toy making.

To my wonderful husband, Nick, thank you for patiently listening to my dreams and helping me to make them our reality. With your support as a partner and best friend, I have been able to accomplish so much in these last few amazing years.

about the author

Erin Freuchtel-Dearing, a longtime crafter and mother of two, is a relative newcomer to the world of woodworking. After the recent scares with toxic and unsafe mass-market toys, Erin decided to turn her attention to making safe wooden toys that also promote creativity. Erin purchased her first scroll saw from Craigslist on a whim, even though she had no prior woodworking experience. With a bit of practice and some help from her husband, Erin was soon able to fill her home with colorful toys—much to the delight of her daughter, Stella, and her son, Elliot. Erin credits her years of experience using a sewing machine for her ability to pick up scrolling so quickly—using the two machines is surprisingly similar. Soon after making that first scroll saw purchase, Imagination Kids Toys was born. Erin and her husband, Nick, design and hand-make toys at their home in Greenwood, Indiana. Their toys have been featured on such outlets as Ohdeedoh, Etsy, iVillage, and Babble. Visit *www.ImaginationKidsToys.com* for more information.

contents

introduction

This book is filled with an array of toys that are sure to delight your little ones. Creatures from the forest, the ocean, the farm, and elsewhere dwell in these pages, merely awaiting your decision to create them—they are quick to cut and can be painted simply or with lots of detail, depending on your style. With the use of some simple tools—a scroll saw, band saw, or coping saw, and some sandpaper—you'll be able to create these straightforward toys in a snap. You'll find here all the knowledge required to create simple but handsome toys that will encourage your child's imagination, with the added plus of knowing the toys are safe and will not be recalled by the manufacturer!

Creating your own natural and safe wooden toys is as easy as following these steps:

1. Attach or trace the patterns onto the wood.
2. Cut along the pattern lines using a scroll saw, coping saw, or band saw.
3. Sand all edges and faces of the toy using a palm sander or sandpaper.
4. Add color, using non-toxic paints or natural dyes.
5. Add details with a woodburner or non-toxic paint.
6. When the pieces have dried, gently sand to smooth any raised grain.
7. Apply wood polish. Wipe away any excess.

A WORD ABOUT TOY SAFETY

Please use your best parental wisdom when deciding which toys are safe for your child. If you have concerns about your child choking on a small toy, remember that all the toys in this book can be enlarged to whatever size you like. Also keep in mind that toys with parts such as wheels and axles could come apart if not constructed properly and attached with plenty of glue. If you are worried about this, remember that any wheels and axles can be omitted as you create the toys. Use your best judgment and knowledge of your child's behaviors to make the safest choices for your family.

Creating these toys is really that easy! And there is a staggering array of projects to choose from:

animals

Foxes

Rabbits

Squirrels

Bears

Hedgehogs

Chickens

Horses

Cows

Pigs

Seahorse

Whales

Crabs

Fish

Dolphins

Turtles

people

Fairytale royalty

fantasy creatures

Dragons

Unicorn

Mermaids

stackers

Cave

Hill

Nature

Haystack

Volcano

Sand dune

Wave

Fountain

vehicles

Tractor

Truck

Sailboat

Car

Helicopter

Airplane

Train

buildings

Castle

Treehouse

Barn

City skyline

plants

Season tree

Mushrooms

Seaweed

Hay bales

Cornstalks

Trees

wands

the advantages of open-ended toys

When a toy has no set purpose, children can use it over and over throughout childhood; this type of toy is called an open-ended toy. To illustrate the point, consider the difference between a traditional board game and a wooden animal, such as those found in this book. The board game has certain rules that must be followed in order for the game play to function properly—there is no room for children to make their own rules or exercise their imagination. However, the wooden animal creates endless play opportunity—the animal could be traipsing through the woods, or be the pet of the princess of some far-away land, or be a game piece in an original game the children create themselves, etc. Open-ended toys inspire children to think and play creatively. Encouraging the development of imagination is one of the best gifts you can give your child.

Simple open-ended toys can be used in countless ways during play. Because a child's imagination is the only limit, an open-ended toy can be an engaging companion throughout a child's early years.

For example, take simple wooden blocks. Babies can enjoy blocks by using them to mouth and chew. Unfinished, well-sanded wood makes for a great natural teething toy. As babies grow, stacking and knocking down blocks can help them to learn about cause and effect. Those same blocks can be used to build castles, cities, or anything else your child's imagination can conjure up as childhood progresses.

Stackers (such as the one featured on page 88) are another wonderful example of an open-ended toy that will grow with your child. At its most basic, a stacker can be used as a simple puzzle that lays flat on the ground. As the child grows, it can become a standing puzzle that helps develop fine motor skills. Finally, as the child's imagination starts to bloom, the stacker will take on a variety of uses—tunnels, caves, hills, haystacks, and more— the possibilities are endless!

By choosing to give your children open-ended toys, you are choosing to allow their creativity to flourish through play.

PLAYSILKS

Another popular Waldorf open-ended toy is the playsilk. These are simply colorful cloths that could be used for endless purposes. Whereas a fairy costume will only ever really be a fairy costume, green playsilks could be the wings of a fairy one day, and the next become a colorful field for wooden toys to romp on, or a handful of flowers, or even a plateful of yummy vegetables! To provide playsilks for your child, simply cut and hem large squares (about 2' [610mm] square is a good size) of solid-colored fabrics, or try searching *www.Etsy.com* for the keyword "Playsilk."

the benefits of homemade vs. store-bought toys

We have all heard the news stories about unsafe toys finding their way into children's hands. From bisphenol A to PVC phthalates to cadmium, plastic and store-bought toys have increasingly been found to contain toxic components.

Phthalates are added to plastic products to make them pliable and soft—items such as teething rings, bath toys, and other flexible plastic toys could contain this chemical. Because phthalates are added to plastic but are not chemically bound there, it is easy for them to leach out of the object, and they may be absorbed when children chew, suck, or play with the object. Some studies have linked phthalates to damaged sexual development.

Bisphenol A, or BPA, is a chemical used during production of polycarbonate plastics and epoxy resins. Examples of some items that could contain BPA include baby bottles and other harder plastic toys. The National Toxicology Program categorizes BPA as an endocrine-disrupting chemical that has some effects on the brain, behavior, and prostate gland of fetuses, infants, and children.

Lead is a well-known health hazard that can be found in paints on some imported toys, and also in some plastics. Lead softens the plastic and keeps it flexible, much like phthalates. The Center for Disease Control and Prevention has stated that the bond between lead and plastic breaks down when exposed to sunlight, air, and cleaning detergents to form a dust that can be easily ingested by children when the toy or object is placed in the child's mouth.

Cadmium is a toxic metal determined by the Department of Health and Human Services to be a known carcinogen. Cadmium can inhibit children's brain development, much like lead. Kidney, lung, and bone damage are also possible.

Natural wood does not contain these harmful substances or additives. Creating your own toys is an ideal way to ensure that you know exactly what your children are playing with. There will be no doubt in your mind that you are providing a safe and stimulating play experience when you have hand-selected all the materials yourself. In addition to wood itself being free of frightening chemicals, you have a few choices of child-safe finishes for your toys. Non-toxic paints (certified by the Art and Creative Materials Institute) are easy to find, colorful, and simple to apply. Better yet, stains made from spices, fruits, and vegetables offer a natural finish. Top either off with a homemade beeswax polish to keep the color fresh and the wood in good condition, while still avoiding dangerous chemical-laden finishes.

From an eco-conscious point of view, wooden toys are simply a better choice for the Earth. They are constructed from a renewable resource and, unlike plastic, can be returned to the Earth after they have worn out. Wooden toys are also typically more durable than their plastic counterparts, which helps to reduce the amount of broken toys heading to the landfill.

Another advantage of wooden toys is that they don't require an endless supply of expensive batteries. Just imagine your home without the obnoxious beeps, chirps, and flashing lights that are so common with modern plastic toys. This is a definite benefit on the days you have a headache or just want a bit of peace and quiet!

about waldorf education

Waldorf education was developed by Rudolph Steiner in 1919, and is based on encouraging a love of learning, self-awareness, and concern for other human beings and the world. The Waldorf method focuses on educating the whole child—not only the intellectual, but also the physical, spiritual, and emotional aspects. Waldorf schools tend to accentuate the creation and appreciation of music, art, and natural objects. Subjects are taught in a different order than in traditional schooling, so as to follow the natural developmental stages of the child. Customarily, one teacher will have one class the whole way through their elementary and middle-school level educations, so as to foster a real bond between student and teacher. The overarching goal of Waldorf education is to foster the internal love of learning present in all children. There are more than 900 Waldorf schools present throughout 83 countries.

There are several easy ways to incorporate Waldorf philosophies into your child's education. Crafting open-ended toys is the method that this book focuses on. Open-ended, natural toys are a fundamental element in the Waldorf tradition, as they encourage the development of imagination, creativity, and love of learning. Waldorf schools hold that imagination is central to the healthy development of any person. Teaching children with nature is another keystone concept in the Waldorf tradition—it is important to expose children to nature throughout their lives. Natural objects play a vital role in awakening the child's wonder for the beauty of life. The celebration of seasonal festivals is another Waldorf tradition, which encourages children to connect with the rhythms of nature and our natural world.

nature tables

While children are out and about in nature, they are bound to find little treasures. My own children enjoy filling their pockets or small bags with stones, leaves, acorns, flowers, shells, and pinecones, depending on the season. A nature table is a place to store all the treasures your children have found, and a way to bring the outdoors into your home and keep nature in your child's life every day. There are many fun ways to embellish your nature table. Try adding wooden figures, stackers, and even playsilks to your nature finds to make a lovely forest, ocean, or other nature scene. There is no need for a nature table to be elaborate; a simple flat space with enough room to keep a few items is perfect.

the basic steps

The projects in this book all follow these simple steps. A few of the toys have

some additional steps that are clearly marked in the projects; however, if

you don't see any special steps, you can assume the toy can be created by

following these steps.

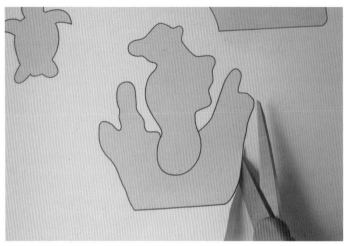

1 **Photocopy and cut out the pattern.** Make a copy of the pattern. Use scissors to carefully cut out the pattern.

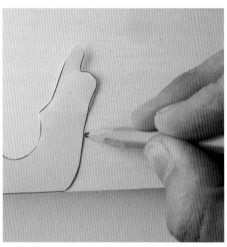

2 **Trace the pattern.** Place the pattern on the wood and trace around it with a pencil.

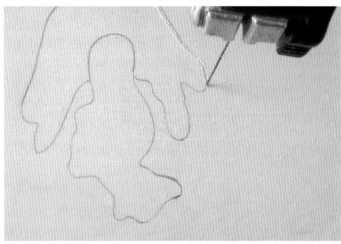

3 **Cut out the toy.** Cut along the pattern lines using a scroll saw, coping saw, or band saw.

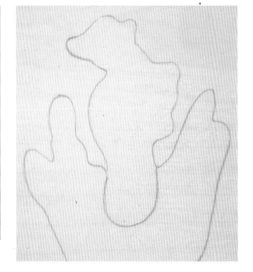

4 **Sand the toy.** Sand all edges and faces of the toy using a palm sander or sandpaper.

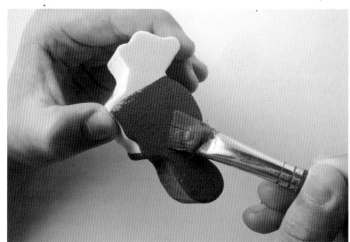

5A **Paint the toy.** There are two choices for adding color to your toys. The first is to use a non-toxic acrylic paint (see page 40). Paints work well on both solid and multi-color pieces. Apply paint with the grain for best results.

5B **Dye the toy.** The second choice for adding color is to apply a natural dye (see page 44). Stains are best for coloring an entire piece, as they tend to bleed along the grain.

PART ONE: GETTING STARTED

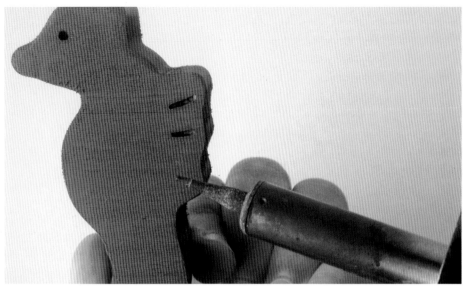

6A **Woodburn the details.** There are two ways to add details to the toy. The first is to use a woodburner to burn in the details.

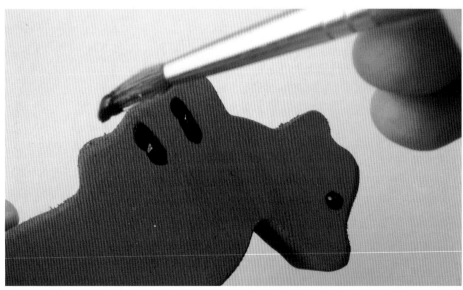

6B **Paint the details.** The second way is to use non-toxic acrylic paint and a fine brush to add details.

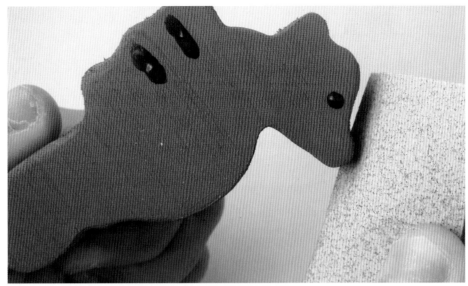

7 **Smooth raised grain.** When the piece has dried, gently sand it to remove any raised grain.

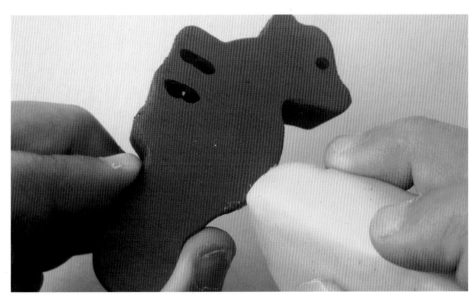

8 **Apply natural finish.** Finally, apply natural beeswax and oil finish to the toy (see page 60).

natural **wooden toys**

wood selection

One of the most important steps in creating beautiful heirloom-quality toys is wood selection. Wood species is important to consider because of the inherent qualities of each species—such as workability (hardness) and color, if you're not finishing the piece. No matter what species you select, though, there are a few general points to check for to make sure the wood will stay in good shape for years to come.

necessary qualities

The majority of the projects in this book are made with ¾" (19mm)-thick stock with a maximum width of 6" (150mm). When you are wood shopping, inspect pieces for any warping, gouges, cracks, or moisture damage. Avoid wood with too many knots, as they will need to be worked around due to their hardness and may take away from the appearance of the toy. Think of your wood as an artist's canvas; you want your canvas to be smooth and defect-free.

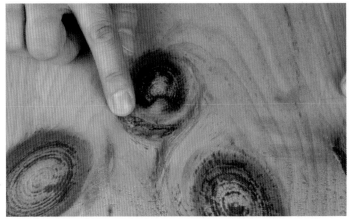

Knots, like the ones pictured here, cause problems when scrolling due to their hardness. It is best to avoid knotted wood.

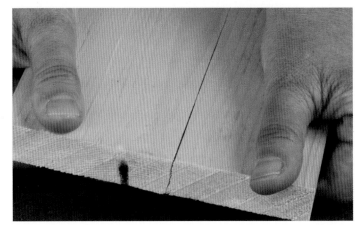

Splits and cracks in a board are not a good sign. You want a nice, flat, intact board when selecting wood.

Basswood, a popular carving wood, is known for its lack of strong grain lines and makes an ideal wood for painted toys.

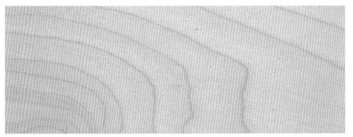

Poplar is a smooth and light-colored wood ideal for finishing with colorful stains and paints.

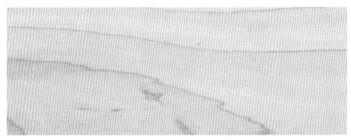

Maple has a light color and is a great base for paint.

Tupelo is a favorite of power carvers, but the light color is great for staining too.

ideal species for painting and staining

There are several varieties of wood that work well for making toys that will be painted or stained. The key trait when picking wood for such a toy is a light, neutral color. That way, when you paint your newest creation, the color will be true. Wood destined to be used in a painted toy should also be smooth and free of knots for easy painting. Aspen, poplar, clear pine, and basswood are light in color, inexpensive, easy to work with, and provide vibrant colors when painted.

brown and caramel woods

Many of the projects in this book, such as the bears, horses, and hedgehogs, lend themselves to beautiful brown- and caramel-hued woods such as walnut, cherry, teak, and others. The natural warm shades of these woods are beautifully rich and strikingly suited for portraying natural animal coats—no paint needed. Simply cut out the figure and woodburn any details, such as eyes and noses.

Walnut is perfectly suited for darker brown toys, such as the bears.

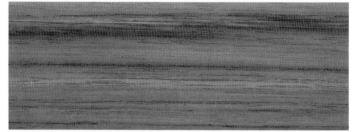

The lovely golden hue of teak could be the perfect choice for a haystacker.

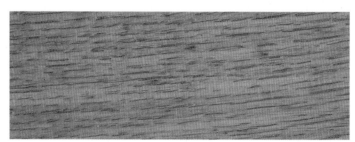

Oak can be a bit tough to cut, but can have beautiful color.

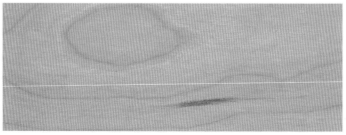

Cherry has a natural reddish brown shade to it.

Purpleheart's purple shade would make for a colorful wand topper. *Photo courtesy of Abarmot.*

The orange color of paduak is very striking.

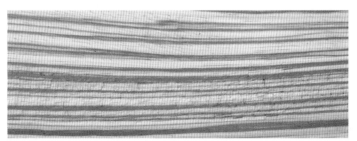

Zebrawood has a fantastic grain that would be perfect for transforming a horse pattern into a zebra!

exotic species

More colorful exotic woods, like purpleheart or padauk, look lovely as star toppers for wands. There is no need to paint these woods, as their beauty is found in their natural state. Keep your eyes open—you never know when you will see the perfect piece of wood for a toy. Browse your local wood store and see if any particular wood catches your attention. Even small odds and ends can be put to use as woodland creatures or wand tops, so see if the shop has a scrap bin. Let your mind wander and see what your imagination comes up with.

other wood parts

A few projects in this book call for additional wooden items such as dowels, wheels, and axles. These items can typically be found in woodworking shops, craft stores, or hardware stores. If you are unable to find these items locally, there are also sources available on the Internet.

selecting and preparing limbs

Natural limbs are used for the tree house (page 96) and seasonal tree (page 98). Find fresh-cut limbs of the correct widths and cut them to size. There are two ways to dry the limbs and prevent the growth of fungus or mold. You can store the wood in a dry, well-ventilated area until it is dry, turning the pieces every few days so they dry evenly. The other option is to bake the wood on a foil-covered baking sheet at 200° or less. Bake for three to five hours, rotating occasionally. You will notice the dried wood is considerably lighter. Gently sand any rough areas and finish with wood polish if desired.

1 **Cut the limb.** Find fresh-cut limbs of the correct widths and cut them to size.

2 **Cover a baking sheet with foil.** Place the limbs on the baking sheet.

3 **Bake the pieces. Bake the wood at 200° or less for three to five hours.** Be sure to rotate or flip the wood occasionally.

4 **Sand the pieces. Let the wood cool.** Gently sand the limb pieces to smooth any roughness.

5 **Finish the pieces.** Use a natural beeswax and oil polish to finish the dried limbs.

tools

The projects in this book can be made using just a few relatively common tools: a scroll saw, a palm sander, and in a few cases, a drill. A bandsaw or coping saw (see sidebar on page 30) can be substituted in place of a scroll saw in most of the projects. The goal of this book is to keep toy making as simple as possible. You don't need a garage full of specialty tools to make creative and fun wooden toys.

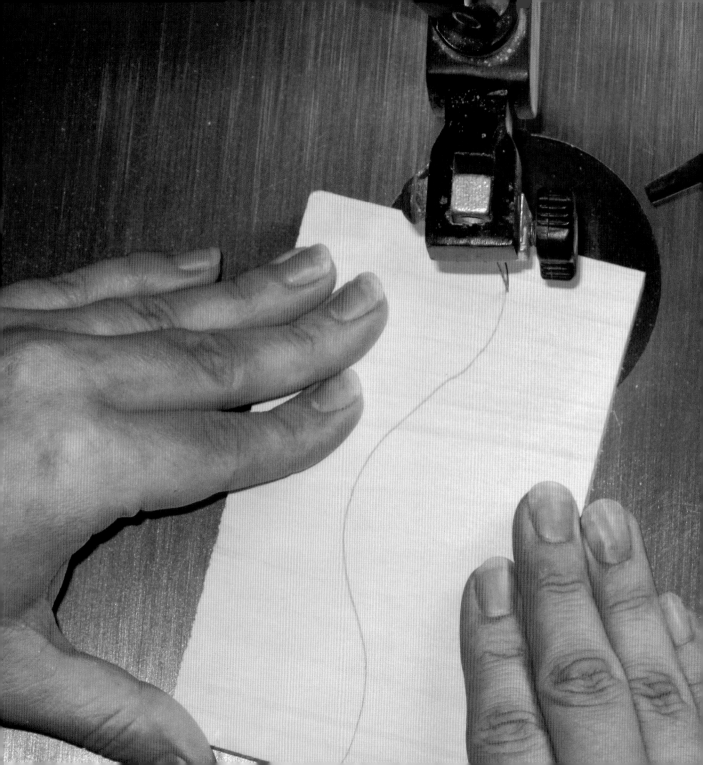

scroll saw

There a few important features to look for in a scroll saw. First is the saw's throat depth. The throat depth is the distance between the blade and the rear frame. The typical throat depths you will find are 16" and 18" (405 and 460mm). Both sizes will be adequate for all the projects included in this book.

Another consideration is how the speed of the saw is controlled. In older scroll saws, it is common to find the saw only has one or two speed settings.

Newer models typically have variable speeds. Variable speed saws give you more control of the blade speed and allow you to slow down a bit for detail work. For most projects, you will be using a medium blade speed.

You also want to make note of the blade-tensioning system the saw has. There are two types of blades available for scroll saws—pin-end blades and plain-end blades. Plain-end blades are available in a greater variety than pin-ended. However, pin-end blades are a bit easier for the novice to install correctly. Some scroll saws have a blade tensioning system that allows for the use of both pin-end and plain-end blades.

using a coping saw

If you don't own a scroll saw, you can still create the toys in this book with the help of an inexpensive coping saw. A coping saw has a thin, easy-to-replace blade that fits inside a metal frame. Make sure the blade's teeth point toward the handle—the saw cuts on the pull stroke. To saw the ¾" (20mm)-thick wood used in this book, you'll want blades with 10 or 15 teeth per inch (TPI).

Cutting curves with a coping saw is easy to do after you learn the techniques. The most important thing to remember is to keep the blade square to the wood's surface. If you don't do this, the sawn edge will be slanted. Practice turning the blade in the handle to get the best sawing angle—you can adjust the blade to whatever angle is needed.

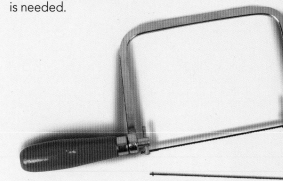

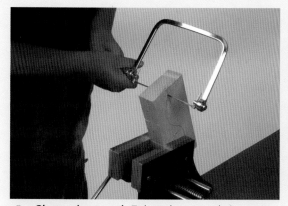

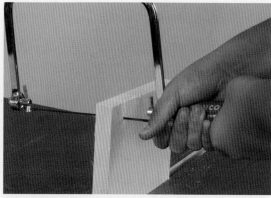

1 **Clamp the wood.** Either clamp on the waste area of the wood or sandwich the wood between two thinner pieces of scrap wood to protect the final wood surface. Use a bench vise (as seen here) or a work table (as shown in Step 2). With both hands holding the coping saw, make short, light cuts.

2 **Follow the outline.** When the blade is started, use the full length of the blade to saw as you follow the pattern line. There's no need to cut speedily—continue slow and steady until you get the hang of it.

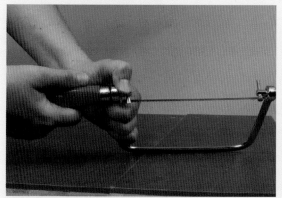

3 **Turn the blade.** As you follow the pattern outline, chances are you will need to move the saw's frame out of the way at some point. When this happens, simply loosen the handle, twist the frame and blade until they're in the position you want, and retighten. Make sure the blade itself is not twisted, or you'll break it.

4 **Continue cutting.** You can see here that the blade's teeth are still following the line, but the frame is handily off to the side. Complete your cutting, pausing to turn the blade as often as needed.

natural wooden toys   31

palm sander

You can sand by hand, but an easy way to speed up the process and achieve a smoother finish is to use a palm sander. Palmer sanders are not terribly expensive and will shorten your sanding time considerably. A palm sander is a small hand-held power tool. It has a pad of sandpaper attached to a flat face that moves.

While browsing the sandpaper aisle, you will note there are numerous grits available. The lower the number of the sandpaper, the coarser the grit. A good grit to use for the initial sanding is 150. When you finish-sand after painting, try using a fine-grit sanding sponge. They are gentle enough to not remove paint if used carefully, but will still remove any rough grain raised by the painting process.

If you're making one toy at a time, you can easily clamp the project you're working on—just make sure to put scrap wood on both sides of the toy. However, if you're making a whole bunch of toys in one go, you may want to consider making the palm sander holder (see sidebar at right). Clamping the sander instead of your toys will save you time when making a large batch.

palm sander holder

Making a mount for your palm sander is an inexpensive, low-impact method for beginner woodworkers to accomplish fine sanding. One of the biggest benefits to mounting your sander is doing so allows you to have both hands free while you sand. The use of both hands is particularly useful on larger items, such as the castle and barn. Mounting the sander also allows more precise sanding of little items, such as the smallest pieces in stackers, or animal figures.

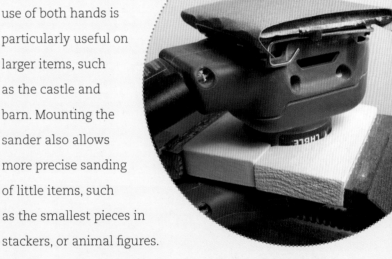

materials & tools

Bench vise

About 6" x 6" (150 x 150mm) piece of wood, depending on your sander

Scroll saw, band saw, or coping saw

Drill (optional)

Screws about 1" (25mm) longer than the short side of the holder half (optional)

Drill bit a little thinner than the screws (optional)

Screwdriver (optional)

1 **Trace the outside shape.** Center your palm sander on the piece of wood, sanding surface side down. Trace around the sanding pad.

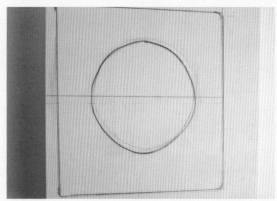

2 **Draw a circle.** Find the narrowest part of the handle and draw a circle a bit larger in the middle of the square you just traced. You will cut this circle away so the handle fits inside the cutout. Draw a line from one edge of the square to the opposite that also bisects the circle.

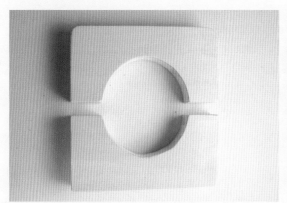

3 **Cut out the holder.** Cut around the square. Next, cut the line that bisects the inner circle—you will have two pieces. Finally, cut out the half circle on each piece. You should now have two pieces of wood that, when put back together, fit around the handle of your palm sander.

4 **Finish the holder.** For extra strength, clamp each piece and drill a hole parallel to the short edge. Make sure to use a drill bit a tad thinner than the screw. Fit the two pieces of wood around the palm sander and insert the screws. Clamp the holder, sanding side up, into your bench vise. Now you are ready to sand.

drill

A few of the projects in this book require the use of a drill to make holes, though none require an extensive amount of drill work. For example, the vehicles need holes for wheel axles; holes are needed to attach the sides of the barn and castle; the seasonal tree needs a hole to install the dowel peg. When looking for a drill, make sure it has variable speeds and a reverse setting. There is an array of drill bit sizes. Drill bits can be bought in assortments or individually. It is nice to have several different sizes on hand, but for this book, you will only need ³⁄₁₆", ¼", and ⁵⁄₁₆" (5, 6, and 8mm).

used tools

Tools can be expensive when buying them all new. One way to help defray some of the initial startup cost is to be creative when tool shopping. Used tools can often be found at garage sales, estate sales, or even Craigslist. If you can, bring along someone who is knowledgeable about woodworking or power tools when looking at used items. Also, don't forget to ask around—there might be a long-forgotten saw tucked away in a relative or friend's garage.

transferring patterns

When you have all your supplies and have picked your project, trace the pattern on a separate sheet of paper or make a photocopy. Then, cut the pattern out along the solid lines. Now you are ready to trace the pattern onto the wood. I recommend using a pencil to trace as lightly as possible. This will cut down on the amount of sanding needed later to remove the lines. It also lessens the chance of leaving indentations from pushing too hard when tracing. You could also use carbon paper. However, it is easy to make homemade transfer paper. Simply shade a piece of paper fully with a pencil, put the colored side down on the wood, place the pattern over the transfer paper, and trace over the pattern.

successful scrolling techniques

One of the most important parts of successful scrolling is knowing your saw. There are numerous variables when using a scroll saw: blade tension, blade type, saw speed, wood type, and wood grain. One of the best ways to get to know your saw is to practice.

blade tension

An important key to having nice smooth cuts and not breaking tons of blades is correctly tensioning the blade. The blade should have very little flex—only about ⅛" (3mm)—when it is correctly tensioned. If you pluck the blade, it should make a "ting" sound. Blades that are too loose can flex from side to side, causing your cuts to be bowed or uneven. Loose blades are also prone to breaking if pressed on too much.

Be careful not to over-tighten the clamps holding the blade, because you can strip the threads in the clamping screw. If the blade keeps pulling loose from the clamping mechanism, try roughing up the ends of the blades and the ends of the clamping screws with a bit of sandpaper.

blade type

Picking out the proper type of saw blade will save you a lot of heartache. I've found crown tooth blades are a great choice for making toys. They leave a smooth edge and handle tight turns quite well for the smaller projects, like animal and people figures.

wood factors

When working with different types of wood, you will find that each species has different characteristics that affect how it cuts. Woods like aspen and pine are on the softer side, and therefore cut a bit easier than harder woods, such as walnut or maple. Hard woods will take longer to cut and dull saw blades more quickly.

Another characteristic to note is the grain of a type of wood, and even of a particular board. Wood grain affects the strength of your project. Pieces that are cut with the grain tend to be stronger than those cut across the grain.

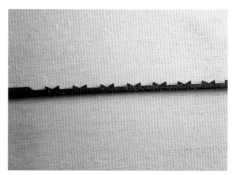

Crown tooth blades work very well for cutting out toys.

general cutting tips

When using your scroll saw, make sure you feed the wood in a smooth and consistent manner. Apply a slight amount of pressure to the wood to keep it in contact with the blade, but be careful to not exert too much. Applying too much pressure on the wood can cause thin scroll saw blades to break or dull quickly.

When preparing to cut, remember the blade does have a bit of flex. This can make cutting a straight line a bit of a challenge—the board must be held at a slight angle to make a straight line. Make sure to feed the wood slow and steady. You shouldn't have to push the wood to make the blade cut. If you are, it's probably time to change the blade for a nice new sharp one, or to slow down a bit.

If you're consistently burning the edges of your cuts, you can correct the problem by applying several layers of clear packing tape over the wood. The packing tape melts as the blade passes rapidly through it, which lubricates the cut and alleviates the extra friction between the blade and the wood. You will most often run into this when cutting harder woods, such as cherry and teak, and when trying to cut corners too quickly.

Push the wood gently against the blade, guiding it slowly along the line.

Due to the way blades are manufactured, it is often necessary to swivel the wood to a slight angle to get a straight line where you want it.

cutting a straight line

The best way to start when learning to use your scroll saw is to practice cutting a straight line. Grab a piece of wood and use a ruler to draw a straight line down the whole length. Line up the pencil line with your scroll saw blade and slowly, on medium speed, begin cutting.

To achieve a straight line, the board must be held at a bit of angle, usually to the left, but experiment with your saw until you find the proper angle. This angle occurs because a side effect of the blade manufacturing process causes one side to be sharper than the other—the blade will take the path of least resistance, thus not cutting perfectly straight. The angle can vary a bit each time you change the blade, but after practicing you will develop a feel for it.

cutting curves

One of the keys to cutting good quality curves is consistency. When feeding the wood, it is important to do so in a slow and steady manner so the cut and curve are consistent and smooth. It may help to look past where the blade is actually cutting so you remain aware and able to anticipate which way to gently guide the wood. It is important to remember that you are turning the wood, not the blade, to keep the blade cutting on the correct path.

cutting tight turns and corners

Corners and tight turns might seem daunting, but don't worry. With a bit of practice and patience, you'll have them mastered in no time. As with all other cuts, slow and steady is the key.

As you approach a tight turn or corner, slow down and have a game plan. Trying to force a tight turn will only result in broken blades and scorched wood from too much friction. Carefully turn the wood so the blade stays on the right path. You can turn the wood quickly, but it must be done in a smooth manner. If you turn the wood too abruptly, there is a good chance your blade will break.

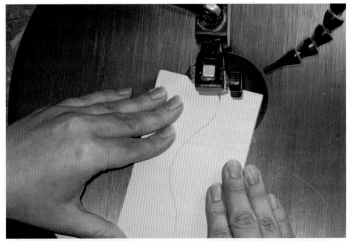

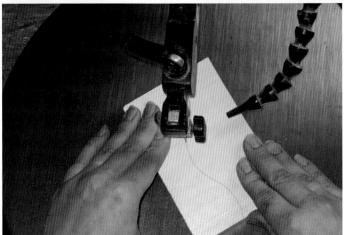

When cutting a curved line, use your hands to turn the wood as needed to keep the blade following the pencil line.

If the turn is in an area with enough waste wood, you can make a small loop in the waste. This loop allows you to turn the wood around and have the blade aligned to cut the other side of the turn.

The loop cut.

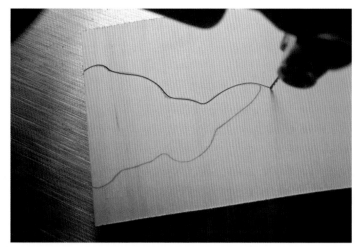

If cutting a tight corner, cut right past the corner into the waste wood.

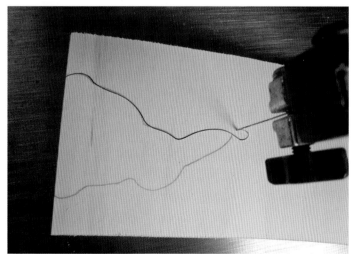

Cut a loop and come back to cut the rest of the line, now coming at it from straight on. Isn't that easy?

practice cutting

A simple and useful way to practice all your new cutting skills is to make a set of blocks. Be creative! Make blocks of all sorts of different shapes: triangles, circles, half circles, trapezoids, squares, or even fun organic squiggly shapes. There is no need to go out and buy wood to make blocks, as scraps of a decent size will work perfectly.

sanding

After your project has been cut, the next step is to sand the edges and corners so they are smooth and safe for little hands. For most projects, 150-grit sandpaper works well for the initial sanding.

A great way to speed up the initial sanding process is to use a palm sander. Instead of time-consuming hand sanding, you can easily and quickly convert most palm sanders into mini sanding stations (see sidebar on page 32).

After painting or dyeing, additional sanding is required for a smooth finish. For this finish-sanding step, use a medium- to fine-grit sandpaper. While sanding this final time, proceed with care so as not to remove any paint or dye. If by accident some paint is removed, just touch it up.

paint

The most important part of selecting paint for toys is making sure it is safe and non-toxic. After you jump that hurdle, there are a rainbow of colors available to deck out your natural toys in kid-safe hues!

safety

When looking for child-safe, non-toxic paint, be sure to look for the Art & Creative Materials Institute's (ACMI) AP certification seal. Products bearing ACMI's AP seal are certified in a toxicological evaluation by a medical expert to contain no materials in sufficient quantities to be toxic or injurious to humans, including children, or to cause acute or chronic health problems. These products are certified by ACMI to be labeled in accordance with the chronic hazard labeling standard, ASTM D 4236, and the U.S. Labeling of Hazardous Art Materials Act (LHAMA).

Conforms to
ASTM D 4236

Image courtesy of ACMI.

The ACMI AP certification seal.

using paints

Acrylic and watercolor are the two most commonly available paints. Both come in a variety of colors. Acrylics tend to be more colorfast than watercolors, but both are good choices.

You can use the color straight out of the tube, or colors can be mixed to create different shades and hues. I suggest diluting the paints a touch so you can see the wood grain through the paint. Diluting the paint also allows the paint to soak into the wood and get a firmer grip so it cannot be easily chipped off.

the color wheel

Keep in mind that you don't need a whole slew of paint tubes to create all the colors you want. Use the color wheel at right to mix any shade you desire from only the three primary colors! Red, yellow, and blue (the biggest dots) are the primary colors. The middle-sized dots between the primary colors are the secondary colors that can be created by mixing the two primary colors to either side of it. Red and blue make purple, red and yellow make orange, and blue and yellow make green. From there, you can create more subtle shades by mixing primary colors with secondaries to create the smallest dot color between them. Don't hesitate to combine secondaries with secondaries, or other primaries with secondaries…you never know what color you'll come up with!

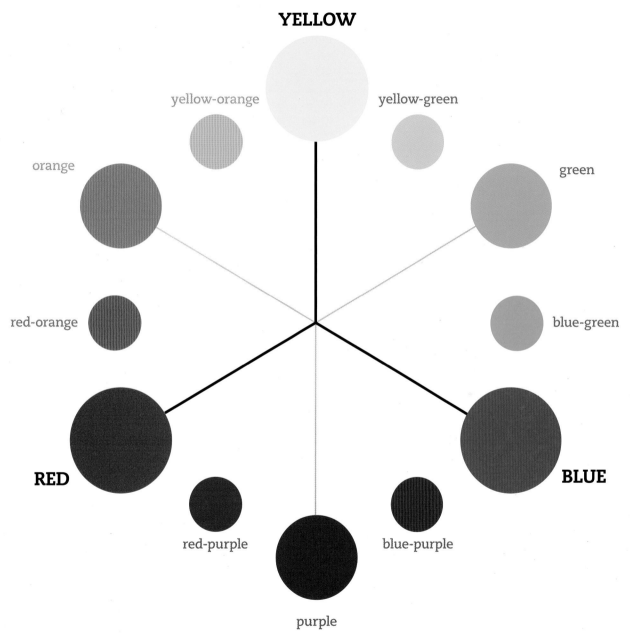

YELLOW

yellow-orange

yellow-green

orange

green

red-orange

blue-green

RED

BLUE

red-purple

blue-purple

purple

natural dyes

Another option for adding color to your creations is staining with natural items, such as berries, spices, and plants. There are a variety of beautiful hues that can be achieved in this manner. The colors produced from these natural dyes will not be as vibrant as paints, but will endow the toy with a soft natural wash of color. Natural dyes are best used for solid colors, not detail work—the dyes tend to bleed a bit with the grain of the wood. Also, natural dyes are not as colorfast as paints, so it is important to make sure you finish dyed toys with beeswax wood polish (see page 60). Most of the following dye recipes are made from common items found in your kitchen or even your backyard. To get the brightest results, be sure to use a lighter colored wood. More than one coat of dye can be applied to make more vivid colors.

Raspberry

Beets

natural wooden toys

Paprika

Turmeric

Spinach

Dandelion leaves

natural wooden toys

Oregano

Red cabbage

Blueberry

Blackberry

natural wooden toys

Coffee

Black tea

spices

There are many spices and kitchen staples that can be used for natural dyes. Here, I've shared a few wood blocks I dyed using turmeric (produces a bright, lively yellow), paprika (a warm orange), coffee (a rich brown), and black tea (a mellow brown). Look through your pantry for powders and granulated items that look bright or dark enough to produce a strong dye.

Turmeric is a source for yellow, as is paprika for orange. To make a dye from turmeric or paprika, you will need ½ teaspoon of the respective spice and ¼ cup of boiling water. Place the spice in a glass bowl and gently stir in the boiling water. When the two ingredients are mixed together and have cooled enough to safely handle, paint the mixture onto the toy, allow it to thoroughly dry, and then brush off any spice residue. Finish with beeswax polish.

1 **Measure out the spice.** Measure about ½ teaspoon of the spice into a glass bowl.

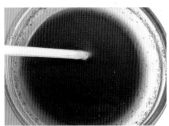

2 **Add hot water.** Boil ¼ cup of water and gently stir into the spice.

3 **Paint on the dye.** Use a paintbrush to apply the dye to the wood.

4 **Wipe off the wood.** After the dye has dried, use a cloth to wipe off any clumps of spice.

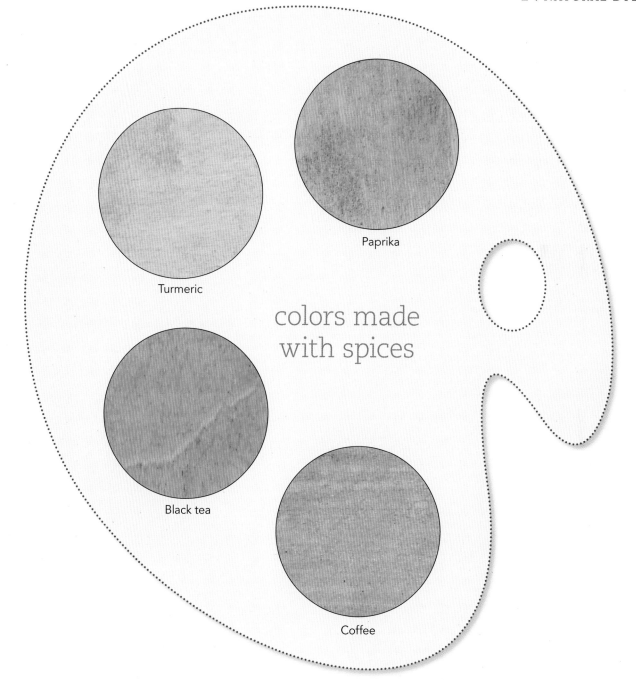

Turmeric

Paprika

colors made
with spices

Black tea

Coffee

berries and vegetables

The majority of bright natural dyes come from the juice of a fruit or vegetable. The best way to create such a dye is to extract the juice from the fruit or vegetable. If the item is juicy, such as a berry, crush it. If the item is a bit firmer, such as a beet or carrot, you'll need to chop it and then soak in water or vinegar. Beyond the examples shown here, you can find more ideas by browsing the produce aisle in your grocery store or farmer's market. If selecting fruit from the wild, it is very important to identify the plant first and make sure it is not poisonous.

1 **Crush the berries.** Put a handful of berries in a glass bowl and crush them. Transfer the berries to a small pot and heat. This extracts more liquid from the fruit.

2 **Strain the juice.** Use a strainer to separate the juice into another bowl.

3 **Paint the wood.** Use a brush to apply the dye to the wood.

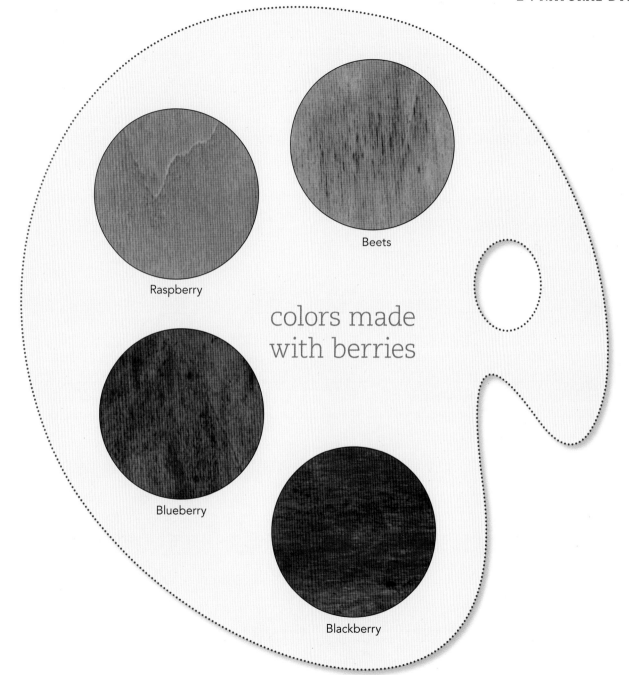

Raspberry

Beets

colors made
with berries

Blueberry

Blackberry

leaves

Leaves are a wonderful source for shades of green. Spinach leaves provide a deep olive green, whereas wild violet leaves give a bright spring green. Feel free to experiment with leaves found in your yard, such as dandelion or grass. Just make sure that the leaves you use are not poisonous. To find information on the safety of different plants, consult a field guide.

The best way to get coloring from leaves is to cook ⅛–¼ cup of fresh leaves with a bit of water until they are soft. Allow the leaves to cool, and then rub the softened leaves onto the wood. When the area has been completely covered, remove any residue. Allow the wood to dry and gently brush off any remaining leaf bits. If you would like a more intense green, repeat the process. When you are satisfied, finish the toy with a light sanding and wood polish.

1 Gather the leaves. Gather about ⅛ to ¼ cup of the fresh leaves you'd like to use.

2 Cook the leaves. Cook the leaves in a bit of water until they are soft.

3 Rub on the leaves. Wait for the leaves to cool. Rub them on the wood.

4 Wipe off the wood. When you've completely covered the area with color, wipe off any leaf residue. Repeat until desired shade is achieved.

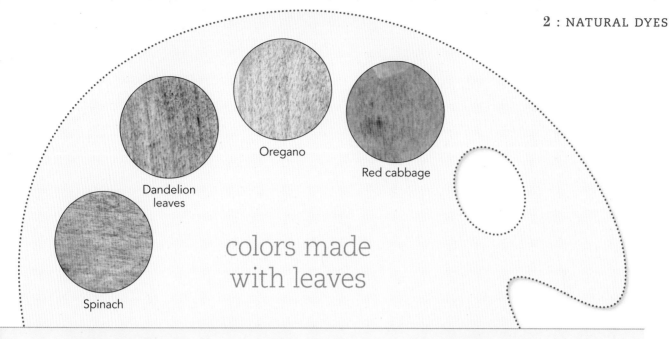

Oregano

Red cabbage

Dandelion leaves

colors made
with leaves

Spinach

raw method

Sometimes, the brightest color dye is produced by simply rubbing the wood on a freshly cut item. For example, I tried using red cabbage as I did spinach, and the sample block was a very light purple. The brilliant shade you see here was accomplished by cutting the cabbage in half and rubbing the block over the cut surface. If you're ever having tough luck producing a bright dye with the boil and rub method, try using the item fresh instead—you may have better luck!

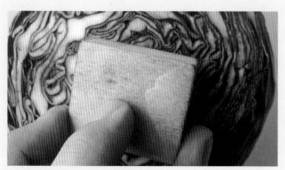

The raw cabbage method.

Red cabbage.

food coloring

Even if you don't have access to fresh produce or leaves, you can achieve vivid colors with the aid of food coloring. Liquid colorings will work, but I recommend the gel icing colors produced by Wilton. Simply mix these with water and go to town! Another option is Kool-Aid—it gives a nice color to light wood. When using food coloring, be sure to apply wood finish afterward, and keep any toys colored this way out of water—this type of dye tends to run when wet.

1 Choose the color. Open the gel container and add a teaspoon to a glass bowl.

2 Mix with water. Mix about ¼ cup of warm water with the gel until fully combined.

3 Paint on the dye. Use a brush to apply the dye to the wood.

Orange

Red

Yellow

colors made with
food coloring

Green

Blue

Purple

natural polish and care

As with paint, when considering the finish for your toys, making sure they are safe is of utmost importance. More often than not, commercially prepared wood polishes meant for items such as furniture are not safe for children. They often contain harsh chemicals and should be avoided, because they are considered to be toxic. There is a simple and inexpensive solution for finishing your toys: make your own wood polish. There are two basic components you will need to make your own polish: oil and wax.

beeswax wood polish

the oil component

I recommend using jojoba oil, but other oils, such as flax and walnut, can be used. Olive oil should not be used because it often turns rancid, giving your toys an unpleasant odor, and could even leave a tacky residue.

the wax component

An inexpensive and eco-friendly wax option is beeswax. You can find beeswax at many craft stores, online, or even at your farmer's market from a local beekeeper. Unlike beeswax, paraffin wax is a petroleum product and is not considered by most to be a natural wax.

adding scent

While beeswax lends a lovely scent to homemade wood polish, you can also add a bit of scent to your polish with a drop or two of an essential oil. Some of my favorite essential oils to use in wood polish are lavender, sweet orange, lemon, and rose. Do not get undiluted essential oil on your skin—it is very strong, and repeated contact could lead you to develop a sensitivity.

All you need to create natural wood polish is beeswax, oil, and an essential oil.

making the polish

Making your own natural beeswax and oil wood polish is very easy. You must first melt the wax, which can be done either in a double boiler or a microwave. Be aware that whatever bowl you use to melt the wax will probably never be completely free of wax residue again—it is best to designate a bowl for wax melting and let it be waxy. After you melt the wax and add the oil and essential oils, allow the mixture to cool completely. The correct consistency is a soft crayon-like thickness, a bit harder than oil pastels.

1 **Melt the beeswax.** There are two basic ways to melt beeswax. The stovetop method requires a double boiler. If you don't have one, you can substitute a glass bowl and metal pot combination. The bowl should fit into the pot, but not touch the inch or so of water in the bottom. If you'd rather use a microwave, dedicate a plastic bowl for wax melting, as the wax can be very difficult to completely remove.

2 **Pour the melted wax.** Put the melted wax into a small glass jar. This will make storage a snap.

3 **Stir in the oil.** Add the oil of your choice. If you are unsure of the consistency of your wood polish, allow the oil and beeswax mixture to cool and test it.

4 **Add essential oils.** If you desire, add a few drops of essential oil. After essential oils are added, do not use a microwave to reheat the mixture. Essential oils can be flammable, and should not be heated in microwaves.

applying the wood polish

Gently rub the cooled polish onto your finished toys with your bare hands. I've found that using a cloth embeds fibers in the finish; additionally, the polish makes a great hand moisturizer! Wipe off any excess polish and your toys are ready to go. Children particularly love helping to wax toys. Let your little ones "color" on the wax and rub it in. Polishing toys together is a great way to teach your children to care for and take pride in their items. If you have leftover wood polish, simply cover the bowl so dust cannot get in.

1 **Rub on polish.** "Color" on the polish so you have a light haze all over the toy.

2 **Rub in polish.** Use your hands to rub in the polish until there are no more chunks of wax left on the surface.

3 **Store extra polish.** If you have polish left over, be sure to seal it up for next time.

wooden toy care

Over the course of play, your wooden toys will probably get a bit dirty. No worries, though, because wooden toy care is not difficult.

Wipe down dirty wooden toys with a cloth and some warm water. If the toys need a deeper cleaning, add a gentle soap (I like Dr. Bronner's). Never submerge or make wooden toys overly wet. This can cause the paint to become distorted or flake off, or even warp the wood. After your toys are dry, reapply a light coat of wood polish to moisturize the wood and protect the finish. Do not use water on food coloring dyed toys, as bleeding can occur. Just wipe those toys with a clean rag and reapply the polish.

1 **Make soap mixture.** Mix some gentle soap with warm water. Moisten a clean cloth with the cleaning solution.

2 **Wipe off any dirt.** Use the wet cloth to rub off any dirt from the toy.

3 **Allow the toy to dry.** Let the toy air dry.

4 **Apply a coat of polish.** When the toy is dry, apply a new coat of natural polish to keep it protected.

natural **wooden toys** 65

1

fairytale

What little one doesn't love to make believe about
castles, dragons, princesses, princes, and a whole host
of other delightful fairytale characters? In this chapter,
you will learn how to create a magical castle, a cast
of characters for your medieval village, a unicorn, a
dragon family and its cave, and various wands for
dress-up play with your little prince or princess.

castle

One of the timeless centerpieces in children's play is a fairytale castle. This wooden castle is the perfect stage for your little ones to spend hours imagining and playing with. The castle folds up so it is easy to store and can be taken on the go. When you cut out the arches, make sure to keep the pieces to use as doors.

tools & materials

Wood, 18" x 8" x ¾"
  (460 x 205 x 20mm)

Strong twine or string, 24" (610mm)

Non-toxic paint or dye, gray and brown

Scroll saw or coping saw

Palm sander or 150-grit sandpaper
  and block

Drill with ¼" (6mm) bit

Paintbrush

Use the patterns on pages 78 and 79.

ADDITIONAL STEPS

Drill the holes indicated on the pattern after the pieces are cut out. After painting the wood, get out the twine. Thread the twine through the holes in the main castle piece. Abut the turret at a 90° angle to the right of the castle, and the squat tower on the left. Thread the twine through the side pieces. Pull both ends of the twine tight and tie 2-3 half hitch knots to secure the castle pieces together.

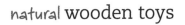

medieval people

No castle is complete without royalty and the king's court. Help the castle come alive by creating inhabitants for the kingdom! The figures are quick to cut out and can be painted any number of ways. This project is a great way to use up any medium- to larger-sized scraps you may have around your shop. Paint is the best option for these wee folks: the high level of detail (faces, fine lines) is not easily created with runny dyes. If you should happen to have a woodburner available, these are perfect projects to try out embellishing with pyrography.

tools & materials

¾" (20mm)-thick wood, various pieces

Non-toxic paint or stains, various colors

Scroll saw or coping saw

Palm sander or 150-grit sandpaper and block

Woodburner (optional)

Use the patterns on pages 80 and 81.

PAINTING TIPS

Your royal court can be detailed any way you like. I recommend using fine paintbrushes while working on these small figures. Also, using lightly drawn pencil lines can guide your painting and help you place details.

dragon pair and cave stacker

Every kingdom needs a dragon to either protect or menace the castle. So whether your knights are out to conquer the dragon or have joined forces with him to fend off invading armies, this is the perfect dragon for you. His removable fire insert allows him to roast imaginary marshmallows, while his small companion dragon keeps him company and gets them both into trouble. The dragon also comes with his own cave stacker, so he has a place to call his own.

tools & materials

Wood, 20" x 6" x ¾"
    (510 x 150 x 20mm)

Dowel, 1" x ³⁄₁₆"-diameter
    (25 x 5mm-diameter)

Non-toxic paint or stains, green, yellow, orange, red, and brown

Scroll saw or coping saw

Palm sander or 150-grit sandpaper and block

Drill with ¼" (6mm) bit

Paintbrush

Woodburner (optional)

Use the patterns on pages 82, 83, and 84.

ADDITIONAL STEPS

After cutting out the big dragon and fire pieces, you'll need to drill the hole for the dowel. Sandwich the pieces separately between scrap wood and clamp them so the mouth of the dragon and the base of the fire are exposed. Drill a hole about ¼" (5mm) deep in each piece. Then, glue the dowel into the fire piece.

unicorn

What fairytale kingdom would be complete without a shining white unicorn for the princess to tame and befriend to become her trusty steed? I painted our unicorn white with a pink mane, but use your imagination and make her as colorful and vibrant as you like!

tools & materials

Wood, 7" x 5" x ¾" (180 x 130 x 20mm)

Non-toxic paint or dye, white, yellow, and pink

Scroll saw or coping saw

Palm sander or 150-grit sandpaper and block

Paintbrush

Woodburner (optional)

Use the patterns on page 83.

wands

These simple and colorful toys will inspire your children to pretend they are part of the magical kingdom you have created for them. Dress up encourages active imaginative play—these wands are a quick and easy way to add to your children's dress up wardrobe. Also, if you are planning a princess, fairy, or other medieval-themed party, these wands make exciting and memorable party favors. Exotic woods, such as purpleheart or padauk, really complement this project. It's also a great way to use up any small scraps around your shop!

tools & materials

¾" (20mm)-thick wood, various pieces

Dowel rod, 8–10" (205–255mm) long and ⅝" (16mm) diameter

Non-toxic paint or dye, pink, yellow, and blue

Scroll saw or coping saw

Palm sander or 150-grit sandpaper and block

Drill with ⅝" (16mm) bit

Paintbrush

Wood glue

Ribbon (optional)

Use the patterns on page 85.

ADDITIONAL STEPS

After you've cut out the wand, drill a hole in its base. After painting, add wood glue to the wand head hole. Insert the dowel rod and ribbon, if desired, and allow glue to dry.

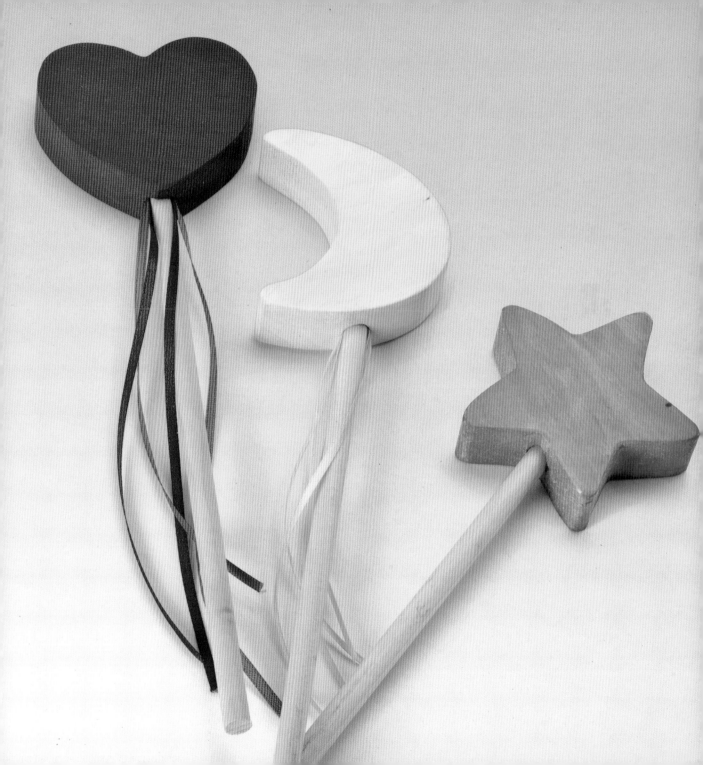

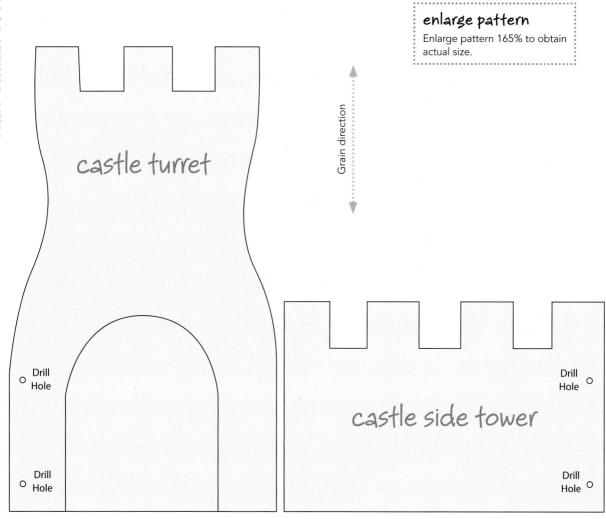

enlarge pattern
Enlarge pattern 165% to obtain actual size.

Grain direction

castle turret

Drill Hole

Drill Hole

castle side tower

Drill Hole

Drill Hole

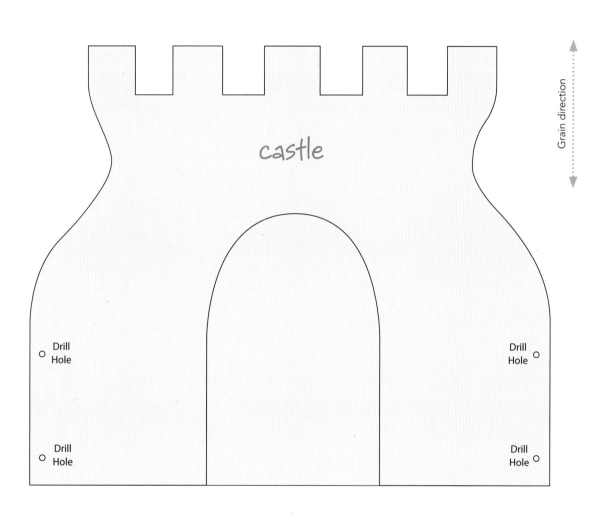

Grain direction

castle

Drill Hole

Drill Hole

Drill Hole

Drill Hole

jester

king

queen

Grain direction

natural wooden toys

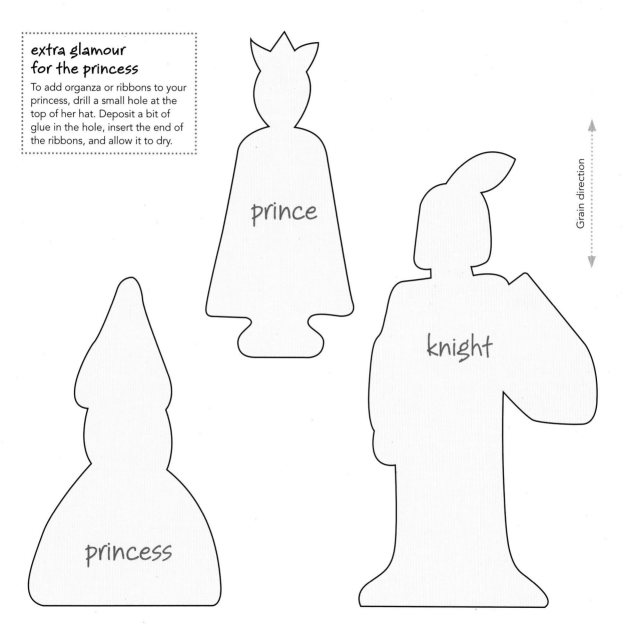

extra glamour for the princess

To add organza or ribbons to your princess, drill a small hole at the top of her hat. Deposit a bit of glue in the hole, insert the end of the ribbons, and allow it to dry.

prince

Grain direction

knight

princess

PART THREE: TOYS

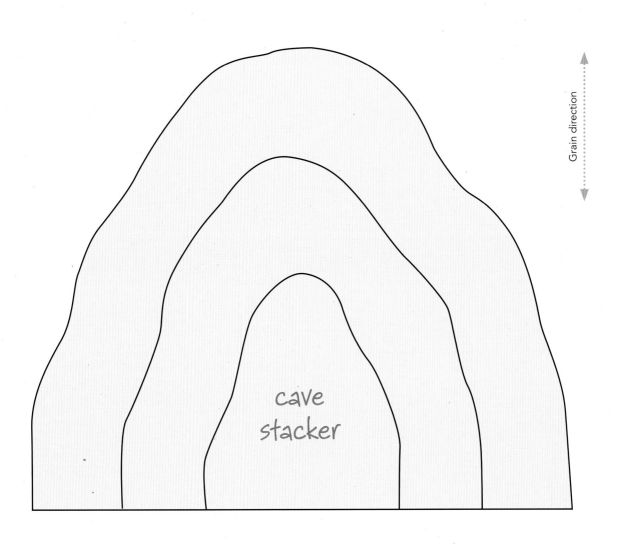

Grain direction

cave
stacker

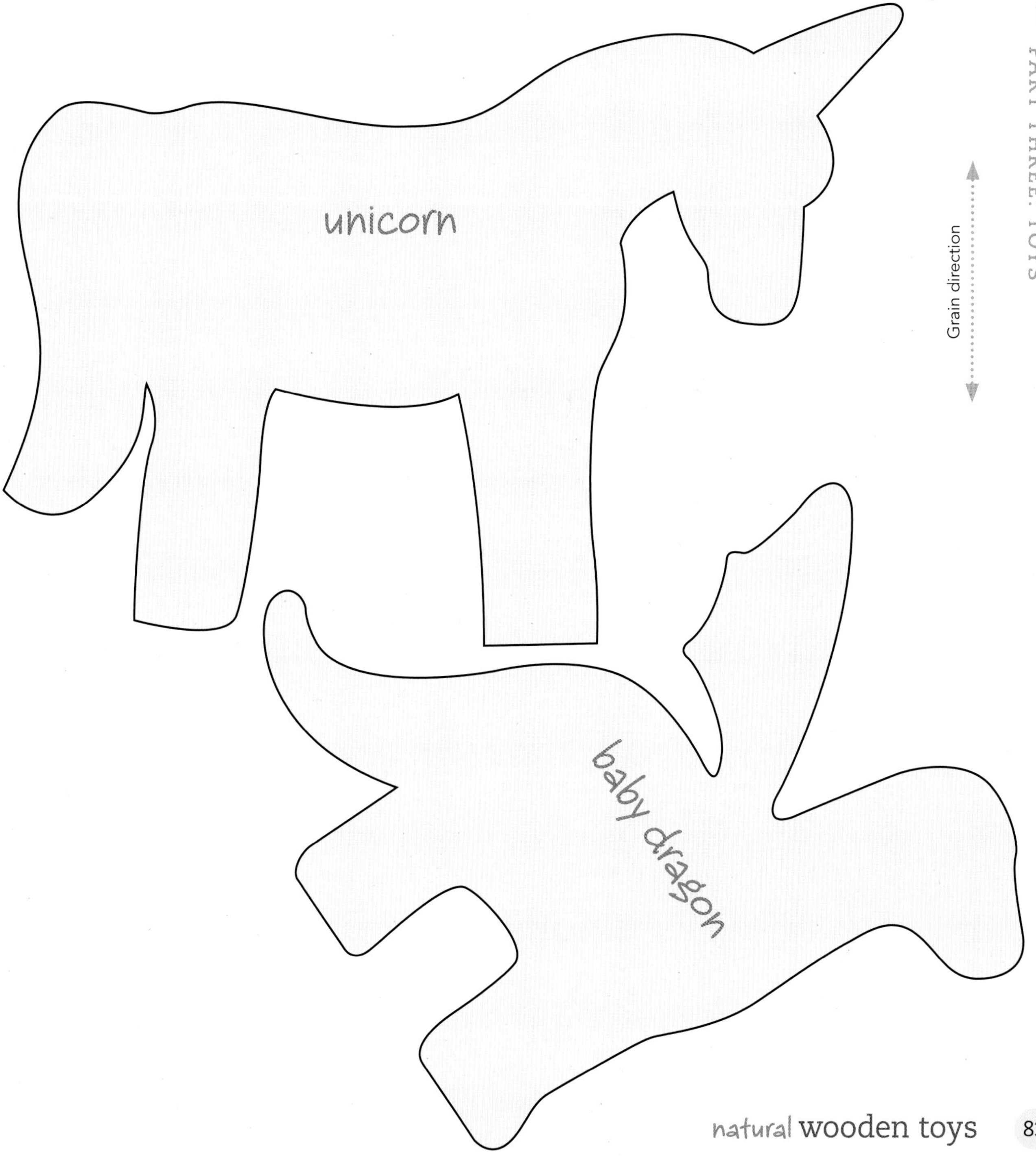

Grain direction

unicorn

baby dragon

PART THREE: TOYS

Drill
Hole

big dragon

Grain direction

dragon flame

Drill Hole

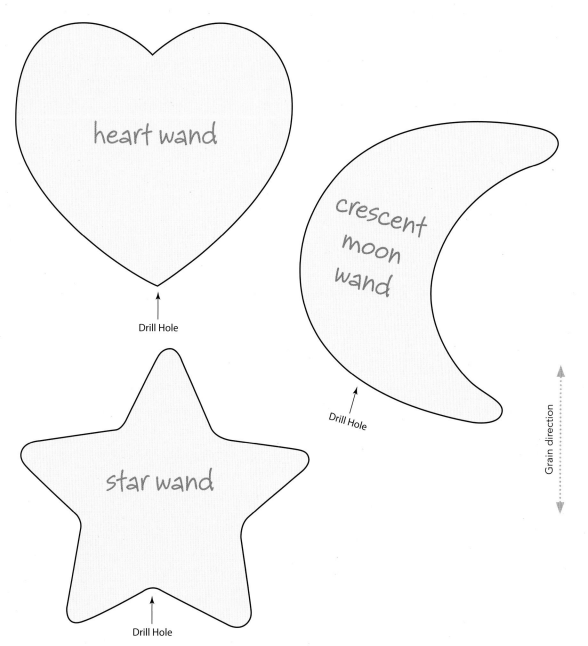

heart wand

Drill Hole

crescent
moon
wand

Drill Hole

Grain direction

star wand

Drill Hole

2
forest

The forest is an enchanting place where bunny rabbits play hide-and-go-seek and hedgehog families frolic among the toadstools. This chapter is full of creatures that hop, dash, and meander about. Create your own cast of fuzzy, furry, and spiky animals—the perfect addition to any child's toy chest. Your kids are sure to love the hill stacker, foxes, bunnies, squirrels, hedgehogs, bears, tree house, seasonal tree, and nature stacker.

nature walk

A nature walk through a forest can be a wonderful family activity. Children can discover the beauty of nature and delight in seeing woodland animals in their natural habitats. Encourage your children to collect stones, pinecones, acorns, and other items that would be great additional scenery pieces to include in their forest play. Ask your child to help find the perfect "trunk" to make a seasonal tree (page 98). Incorporating these natural aspects into their play helps children to get and remain in touch with the natural world around them.

hill stacker

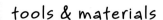

Green grassy hills are the perfect place for bunnies to frolic and hedgehogs to hide. Make your own hill stackers for your forest animals to play in. This is a great project for children to help with because it is easy to trace and simple to paint. It is even a great first cutting project, as the lines are smooth and don't have to be extremely precise.

I recommend using three different shades of green to finish the stacker—that way each arch is a separate vibrant shade.

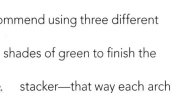

tools & materials

Wood, 5" x 4" x ¾" (130 x 100 x 20mm)

Non-toxic paint or dye, green and yellow

Scroll saw or coping saw

Palm sander or 150-grit sandpaper and block

Paintbrush

Use the patterns on page 102.

PAINTING TIPS

Different shades of green are what give this stacker its charm and grassy feel. The smallest piece is painted the darkest shade of green, while each larger successive piece is a slightly lighter shade of green. To achieve these bright, varied shades of green, paint the center pure green; then add a bit of yellow to the mixture for each successive piece to achieve the desired color.

foxes

These crafty red foxes love dashing through the forest, jumping over logs, and chasing butterflies. If you're feeling creative, try cutting them a den of their very own—use the hill stacker pattern (page 88) as a starting point, but make the den lower and rounder. If your forest needs a big bad wolf, try enlarging the pattern a bit and painting your wolf gray with a patch of silvery fur on the chest, or white and black for a timberwolf.

tools & materials

Wood, 4" x 6" x ¾" (100 x 150 x 20mm)

Non-toxic paint, red, white, and black

Scroll saw or coping saw

Palm sander or 150-grit sandpaper
   and block

Paintbrush

Woodburner (optional)

Use the patterns on page 102.

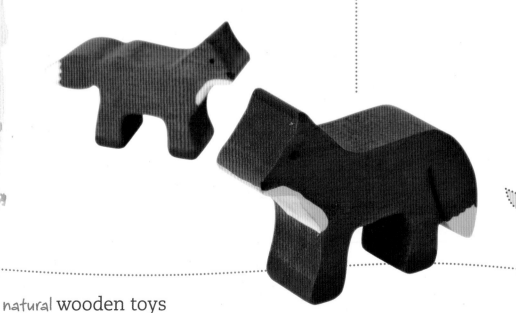

bears

This mamma and baby bear lumber through the forest in search of honeybee hives, sweet berries, and juicy fish. They'd love it if you cut them their very own cave (page 82) to hibernate in, too! Try your hand at scrolling a beehive, or adapt one of the fish on page 153 into a spotted rainbow trout.

tools & materials

Wood, 5" x 6" x ¾" (125 x 150 x 20mm)

Non-toxic paint, brown

Scroll saw or coping saw

Palm sander or 150-grit sandpaper and block

Paintbrush

Woodburner (optional)

Use the patterns on page 103.

bunny family

These happy bunnies hop here and there, wiggling their noses at flowers and nibbling on carrots. If you want to make accessories for your rabbit family, try cutting out a carrot, tufts of grass, and other delicious vegetation. If you're creating an Easter bunny, break out brighter paint and dye colors to make a pink or blue rabbit. For even more fun, cut out wooden egg shapes and help your children dye them with natural dyes (see page 44).

tools & materials

Wood, 6" x 5" x ¾" (150 x 125 x 20mm)

Non-toxic paint, brown and white

Scroll saw or coping saw

Palm sander or 150-grit sandpaper and block

Paintbrush

Woodburner (optional)

Use the patterns on page 102.

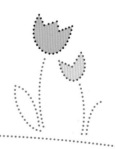

squirrels

This nutty pair will chatter all day from atop their favorite oak tree, and dash up and down the trunk at the drop of an acorn. I like to paint their curly tails a slightly different shade of brown to distinguish them from the coats—try straight brown for the tail and some brown mixed with yellow for the body. If you don't have real acorns in your area, you can always cut one out of wood—and don't forget how much squirrels love other nuts and seeds! This squirrel pair would gladly chow down on corn cobs, walnuts, and even birdseed—try cutting out these other treats, or help your child find the real deal to incorporate into their play.

tools & materials

Wood, 4" x 6" x ¾" (100 x 150 x 20mm)

Non-toxic paint, brown and yellow

Scroll saw or coping saw

Palm sander or 150-grit sandpaper and block

Paintbrush

Woodburner (optional)

Use the patterns on page 102.

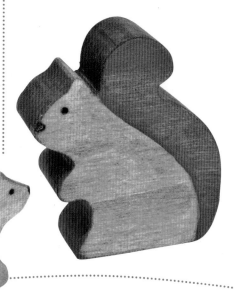

hedgehogs and toadstools

This prickly pair may not look too inviting, but you will

find they're some of the friendliest creatures in the forest.

These hedgehogs love to doze off under their favorite

two toadstools, especially when a patch of warm sunlight

falls just so! The hedgehogs are one of my favorite toys to

make, and I bet your kids will love these little sweeties too.

Get out your bright colors to paint the toadstools!

tools & materials

Wood, 6" x 6" x ¾" (150 x 150 x 20mm)

Non-toxic paint, brown, tan, red, green, and white

Scroll saw or coping saw

Palm sander or 150-grit sandpaper and block

Paintbrush

Woodburner (optional)

Use the patterns on page 103.

tree house

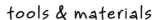

What child doesn't dream of spending their afternoons in a magical tree house deep in the forest? This toy has all the perfect tree house accessories—a rope ladder to climb, a swing to play on, and a table to hold woodland tea parties with all your forest friends. The tree house is sure to be the center of all your child's forest play. For a bit of extra fun, include some small pieces of fabric for your little one to use as blankets or tablecloths, and acorn tops to use as tiny bowls or baskets. See the step-by-step on selecting and preparing limbs on page 26.

tools & materials

Wood, 18" x 6" x ¾"
(460 x 150 x 20mm)

Natural tree limb or dowel rod,
1" (25mm) diameter, 2 pieces

Tree limb slices, 1" (25mm) diameter,
3 or 4 (Rope ladder)

Tree limb or dowel halves, 1½" (40mm)
diameter, 3" (75mm) long, 2 (Bench
and swing)

Tree limb slice, 2½" (65mm) diameter
(Table top)

Tree limb slice, 1" (25mm) diameter,
1" (25mm) long (Table pedestal)

Wooden peg or dowel, ⅛" (3mm) to
hang swing from

1½" (40mm) screws, 4

Twine or heavy duty string, 24" (610mm)

Scroll saw or coping saw

Palm sander or 150-grit sandpaper
and block

Drill with screwdriver bit to match
screws, drill bit a little larger than
twine, drill bit the size of the peg for
the swing

Wood glue

Use the patterns on pages 104 and 105.

additional steps

To attach the pillars to the base of the tree house, start screws from the bottom. Drive each screw through the base until just the top point of the screw is visible on the other side. Place each limb piece so the screw tip is centered on the bottom. Apply a bit of pressure to the top of the limb and continue to drive the screw until it is flush with the base. Attach the top level of the tree house in the same way.

Cover one of the screw heads on the top of the tree house by gluing the two table pieces together and then gluing the table over the screw. Glue the bench over the other screw head.

swing

Drill a hole just large enough to thread your twine through both sides of the swing. Measure the distance from the top of the tree house to where you want the bottom of the swing to hang. Cut two pieces of twine a few inches longer than that distance. Tie two knots on top of each other to make one large knot at the bottom of each string. Drill a hole, using a bit the diameter of the peg or dowel you are using, in the side of the tree house where you want the swing to hang. Put the dowel/peg in place with a bit of wood glue and then tie the swing onto the peg at the length you would like the swing to hang. Trim any excess twine.

rope ladder

Drill a hole in the center of each of the slices of wood for the rope ladder. Measure the distance from the top of the tree house to where you want the bottom of your rope ladder to hang. Cut a piece of twine a few inches longer than that distance. Tie two knots on top of each other to make one large knot at the bottom of the string. This will keep the wood pieces from coming off the twine. Thread one disk onto the twine. Decide where you would like the next step on the ladder and tie another large knot. Add another disk and repeat until all disks are in place.

Drill a hole through the top of the tree house. Thread the ladder up through the hole. Double-check the length of the ladder and then knot the top of the thread so the ladder will be suspended from the top of the tree house. Snip any excess thread from the top and bottom.

seasonal tree

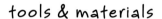

Trees are to forests as skyscrapers are to metropolises, so no forest play set should be without a large tree or two. Help teach your child about the different seasons by using the different interchangeable treetops to illustrate how trees change throughout the year. To create a whole forest, reduce or enlarge the tree top pattern and cut different length trunks to craft various sized trees. You can even use the toppers without a base as bushes. Add a few red dots to create berry bushes for your bears (page 91) to nibble on. See the step-by-step on selecting and preparing limbs on page 26.

tools & materials

Wood, 9" x 6" x ¾" (230 x 150 x 20mm)

Branch or dowel rod, 4-6" (100-150mm) long and 1" (25mm)-diameter

Dowel rod, 1½" (40mm) long and ⅝"(16mm)-diameter

Screw, 1½" (40mm)

Wood glue

Non-toxic paint or dye, various colors

Scroll saw or coping saw

Palm sander or 150-grit sandpaper and block

Drill with ⅝" (16mm) bit

Paintbrush

Use the patterns on page 106.

additional steps

After cutting out the tops, use the drill to make a hole along the edge at the flat part on the treetop.

Locate where you want the trunk of the tree to be located on the base. On bottom of the base, pre-drill a recess in the wood that is large enough for the screw head so the base will sit level when the screw is placed. Place the base at the end of the trunk with the recess away from the trunk. Screw the base to the trunk until the screw head is flush with the base.

Use a ⅝" (16mm)-diameter drill bit and drill a hole ¾" to 1" (20 to 25mm) deep into the top of the trunk. Put a bit of wood glue into the hole and gently tap the ⅝" (16mm)-diameter dowel into the hole.

painting ideas

In the spring, trees come alive with bright green leaves. Try using lively shades of spring green.

As the leaves mature in the summer, they become a deeper shade of green. You can also paint little apples or pears for a bit of color and variety.

Gold, burgundy, and orange are the perfect picks for your autumn treetop. It's best to start with a base coat of the lightest color you will be using, water down the other colors a bit, and then gently blend them to make a colorful tree.

Sadly, during the winter, all the beautiful leaves have gone and all we are left with are the limbs. If you would like to give your trees a snowy touch, use whites and pale blues to paint the treetop. Then, add in limbs by painting them with dark brown or using a woodburner.

nature stacker

This toy is very similar to a classic ring stacker, but with a twist. The largest piece is a sun shape, followed by a flower, a ladybug, and a cloud. Encourage your children to stack the pieces from largest to smallest, smallest to largest, or any other organization they can think of. Don't forget that the pieces are great additions to any forest scene just on their own!

tools & materials

Wood, 18" x 6" x ¾" (460 x 150 x 20mm)

Non-toxic paint or dye, various colors

Dowel rod, 5" (130mm) long and ⅝" (16mm)-diameter

Scroll saw or coping saw

Palm sander or 150-grit sandpaper and block

Drill with ⅝" (16mm) and ¾" (19mm) bit

Paintbrush

Wood glue

Use the patterns on pages 107, 108, and 109.

ADDITIONAL STEPS

To cut the inner circles, drill an entry hole on the inside of where the hole will be. Release the top of the saw blade and thread the blade through the entry hole. Secure the blade again and cut the inner circle out. Repeat for each piece.

Drill a ⅝" (16mm) hole halfway through the base. Add a few drops of wood glue to the drilled area on the base of the toy. Place the dowel rod in the hole. Allow the glue to thoroughly dry.

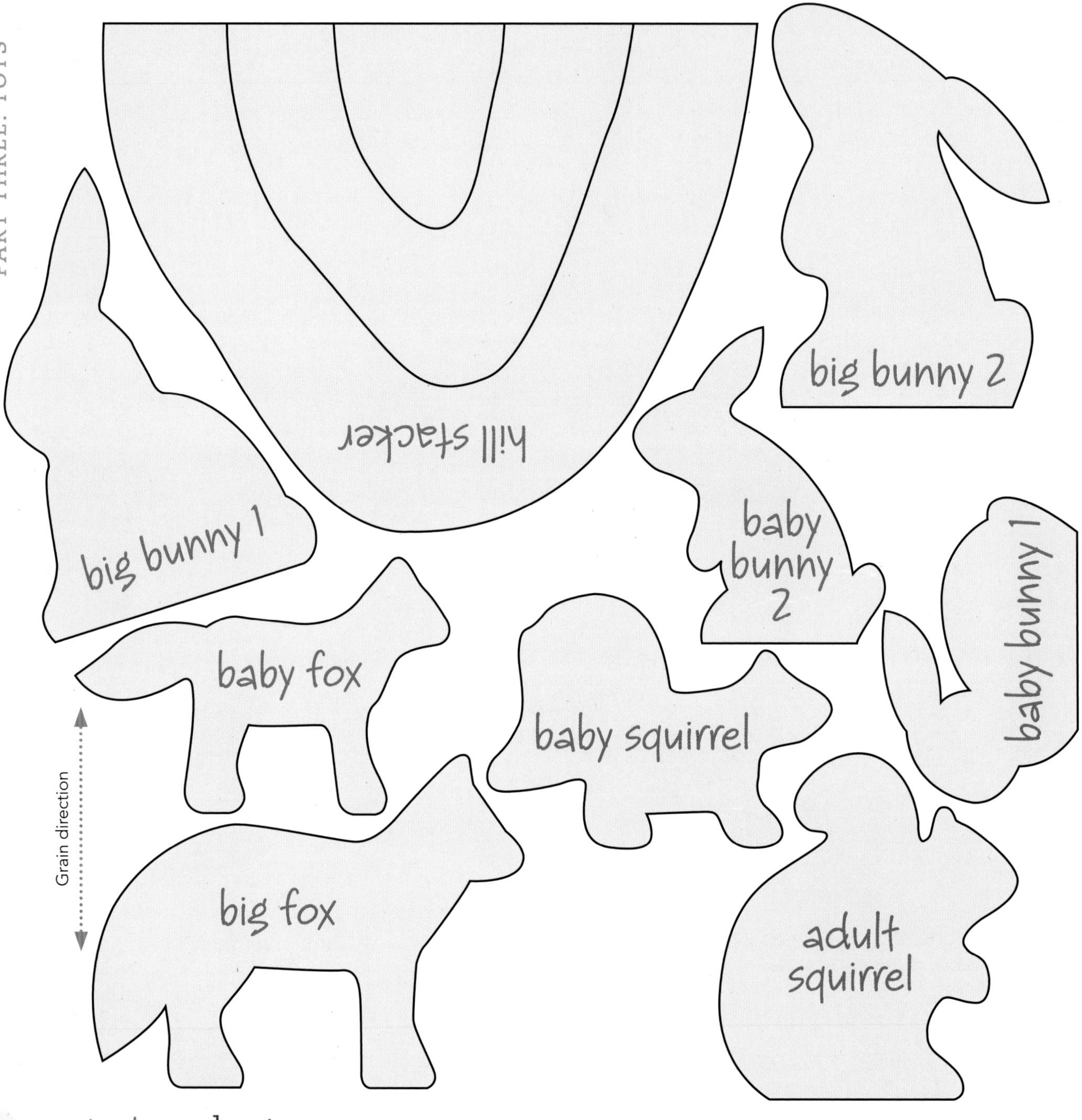

big bunny 2

hill stacker

baby
bunny
2

big bunny 1

baby bunny 1

baby fox

baby squirrel

Grain direction

big fox

adult
squirrel

baby bear

big bear

big hedgehog

baby hedgehog

wide toadstool

skinny toadstool

Grain direction

natural **wooden toys**   103

Grain direction

enlarge pattern
Enlarge pattern 125% to obtain actual size.

lower treehouse piece

Grain direction

upper treehouse piece

Grain direction

tree base

○
Drill
Hole

seasonal tree topper

flower

Drill Hole ¾" (19mm)

cloud

Drill Hole ¾" (19mm)

ladybug

Drill Hole ¾" (19mm)

Grain direction

PART THREE: TOYS

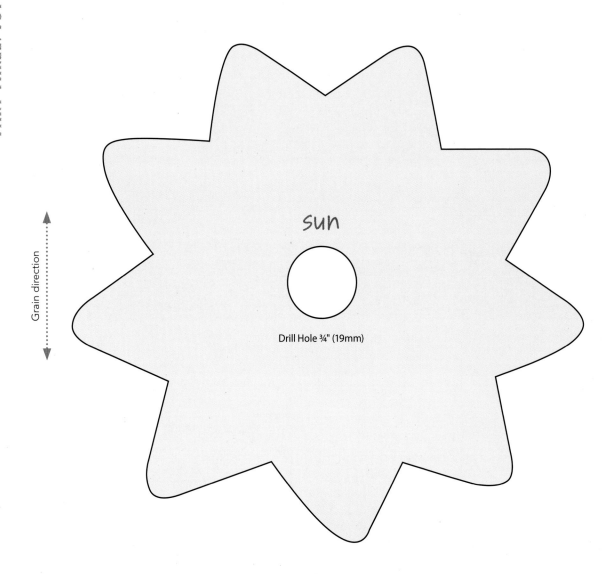

sun

Drill Hole ¾" (19mm)

Grain direction

Grain direction

base

Drill Hole ⅝" (16mm)

3

farm

The farm is a place children love, whether they are riding ponies, running through fields, chasing piglets, or playing hide-and-go-seek in the hayloft. Moo, neigh, cluck cluck, and oink are the sounds of a farmyard coming alive. Those sounds can fill your home too, with the help of your little ones. Wooden animals are quick to cut out and fun to paint. Because of their size they are great on the go, too. They fit well into little pockets or slip them in a purse or diaper bag for plenty of entertainment on a trip or at a restaurant. While taking a trip to the farm might not always be possible, you can always bring the farm to your children.

barn

No farm is complete without a big barn for animals to live in and children to explore. This barn is easy to make and tons of fun. Your barn raising will go quite quickly! No nails or screws needed, just a bit of twine and a few half hitch knots, and your barn will be ready to go!

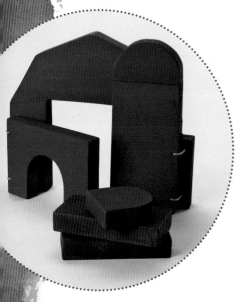

tools & materials

Wood, 18" x 8" x ¾" (460 x 200mm x 20mm)

Twine or string, 24" (610mm)

Non-toxic paint or dye, red, brown, and black

Scroll saw or coping saw

Palm sander or 150-grit sandpaper and block

Drill with ¼" (6mm) bit

Paintbrush

Use the patterns on pages 124 and 125.

ADDITIONAL STEPS

Drill the holes indicated on the pattern after the pieces are cut out. After painting the wood, get out the twine. Thread the twine through the holes in the main barn piece. Abut the silo at a 90° angle to the right of the barn, and the shed on the left. Thread the twine through the side pieces. Pull both ends of the twine tight and tie 2-3 half-hitch knots to secure the barn pieces together.

haystack stacker

Need a place for animals and farm children to play and hide at your farm? This haystack stacker is the perfect thing. The calves and foals can hide in the stacker, and the farm truck can drive through a hay tunnel.

tools & materials

Wood, 5½" x 7" x ¾"
(140 x 180 x 20mm)

Non-toxic paint or dye, yellow and brown

Scroll saw or coping saw

Palm sander or 150-grit sandpaper and block

Paintbrush

Use the patterns on page 126.

PAINTING TIPS

A mixture of yellow and brown paint is perfect for the different pieces of the haystack stacker. The smallest pieces are the darkest shade of tan, with each successive larger piece a slightly lighter shade of gold.

hen and rooster

Cock-a-doodle-doo! This lively pair of chickens will flap and crow around your farm. Maybe the hen will even lay an egg or two! Try your hand at creating a stacked nest for the chickens to sit in.

tools & materials

Wood, 3" x 6 ½" x ¾" (75 x 150 x 20mm)

Non-toxic paint, yellow, brown, and red

Scroll saw or coping saw

Palm sander or 150-grit sandpaper and block

Paintbrush

Woodburner (optional)

Use the patterns on page 126.

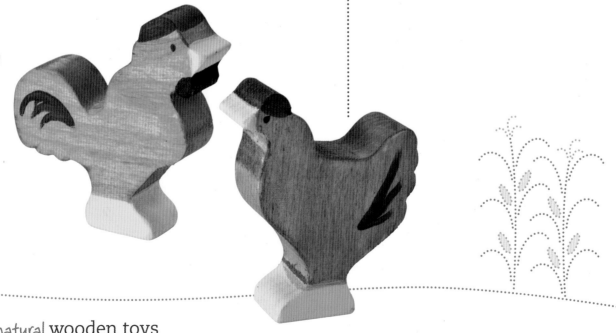

COWS

Moo! By far the most well-known farm animal, cows will add a hoot 'n holler to your down-home farm. If you're ambitious, try scrolling udders on the cow, or add horns to make a bull. Don't forget to get your paintbrush ready to give your bovine friend some spots!

tools & materials

Wood, 4½" x 6" x ¾" (115 x 150 x 20mm)

Non-toxic paint, white and black

Scroll saw or coping saw

Palm sander or 150-grit sandpaper and block

Paintbrush

Woodburner (optional)

Use the patterns on page 127.

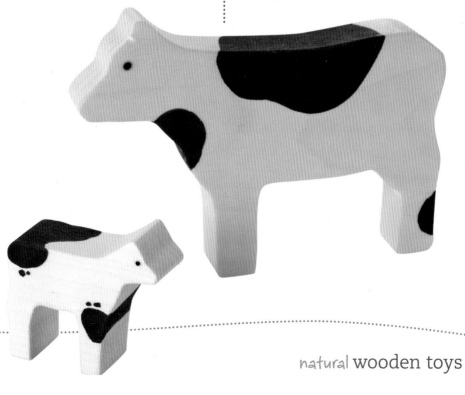

horses

Saddle up! Whether your little one wants to be a cowboy or cowgirl, a professional rider, or a knight in shining armor, they'll be delighted with these little horses. Cut out a whole herd and paint them as different breeds, or even your favorite famous horses.

tools & materials

Wood, 4½" x 6½" x ¾" (115 x 165 x 20mm)

Non-toxic paint, various colors

Scroll saw or coping saw

Palm sander or 150-grit sandpaper and block

Paintbrush

Woodburner (optional)

Use the patterns on page 127.

pigs

These oinkers love poking around in slop and hay, playing in the mud, and showing off their pink noses. Cut a set for your child and see what adventures the piggy pals get into!

tools & materials

Wood, 3″ x 6″ x ¾″ (75 x 150 x 20mm)

Non-toxic paint or dye, pink

Scroll saw or coping saw

Palm sander or 150-grit sandpaper and block

Paintbrush

Woodburner (optional)

Use the patterns on page 129.

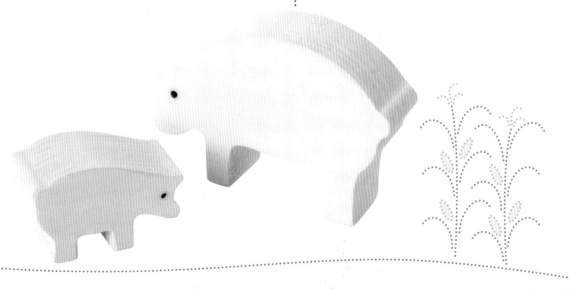

tractor and farm truck

There's a lot of work to be done on the farm, and this tractor and truck are great help with getting the job done. Plow the fields, haul the hay bales, take those eggs to market—your little ones will have a blast zooming about all over the farmyard in their vehicles. Vroom, vroom!

ADDITIONAL STEPS

Drill 2 holes, where shown, in the body of each vehicle. Put a little glue in the holes, and then insert the pegs through the wheels into the holes. Allow to dry.

tools & materials

Wood, 6½" x 3" x ¾" (165 x 75 x 20mm)

Wooden wheels per vehicle, 1½" (40mm)-diameter and ½" (15mm) thick x 4

Wooden peg axles per vehicle, 1¼" (32mm) long with 7/32" (5.5mm) tenons x 4 (You might need to trim a bit off the ends)

Non-toxic paint or dye, various colors

Scroll saw or coping saw

Palm sander or 150-grit sandpaper and block

Drill with 7/32" (5.5mm) bit

Paintbrush

Wood glue

Use the patterns on page 128.

hay bales and cornstalks

To help complete your farmyard play, try making a few hay bales, miniature haystacks, and corn stalks. Throw some of those hay bales on top of the truck; hide the chickens in the corn stalks—the possibilities are endless.

These would also make great additions to your nature table (see page 12).

tools & materials

Wood, 3" x 6" x ¾" (75 x 150 x 20mm)

Non-toxic paint or dye, various colors

Scroll saw or coping saw

Palm sander or 150-grit sandpaper and block

Paintbrush

Woodburner (optional)

Use the patterns on page 129.

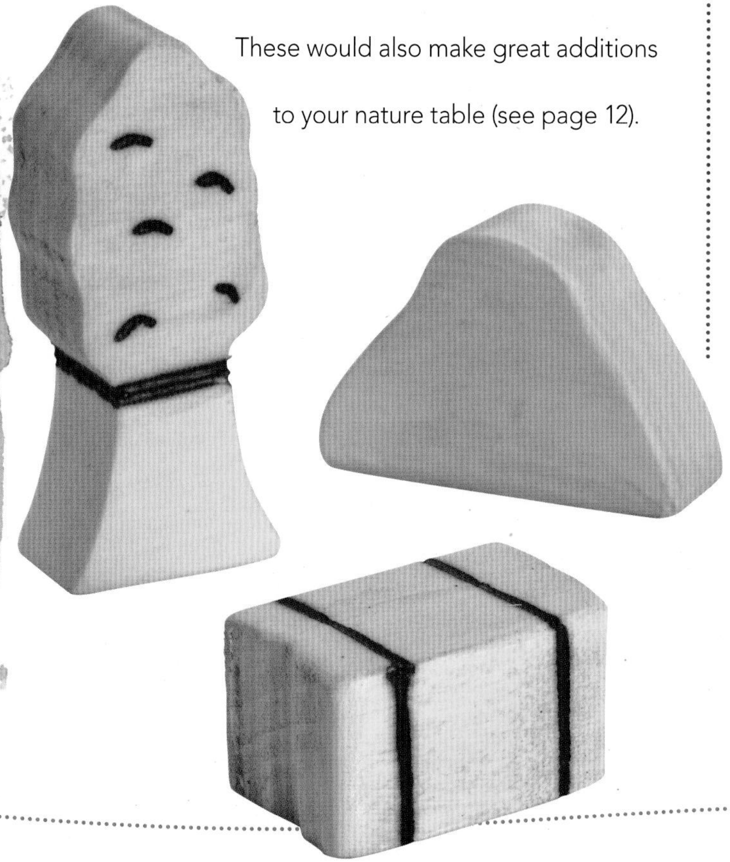

wands

These wands are the perfect way for your children to get in on the barnyard fun in an active way. They can fly their butterflies and ladybugs all over the place. Flutter here and there!

ADDITIONAL STEPS

After you've cut out the wand, drill a hole in its base. After painting, add wood glue to the wand head hole. Insert the dowel rod and ribbon, if desired, and allow glue to dry.

tools & materials

Wood, 4" x 6" x ¾" (100 x 150 x 20mm)

Dowel rod, 8–10" (205–255mm) long ⅜" (10mm)-diameter

Non-toxic paint or dye, various colors

Scroll saw or coping saw

Palm sander or 150-grit sandpaper and block

Drill with ⅜" (10mm) bit

Paintbrush

Wood glue

Ribbon (optional)

Use the patterns on page 129.

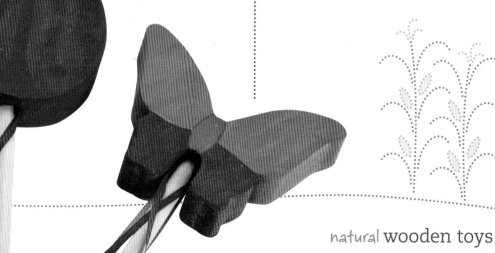

enlarge pattern
Enlarge pattern 125%
to obtain actual size.

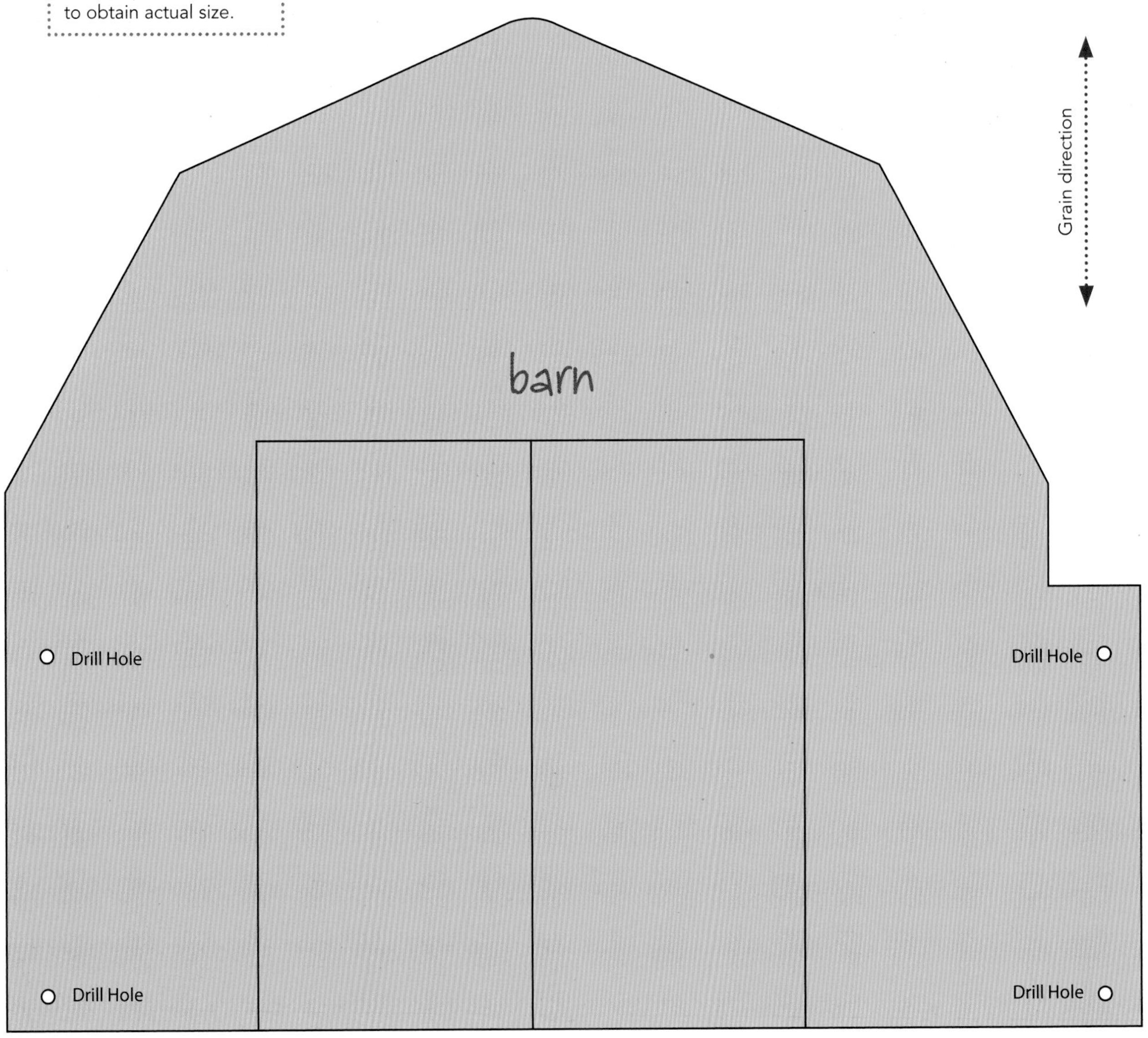

Grain direction

barn

Drill Hole

Drill Hole

Drill Hole

Drill Hole

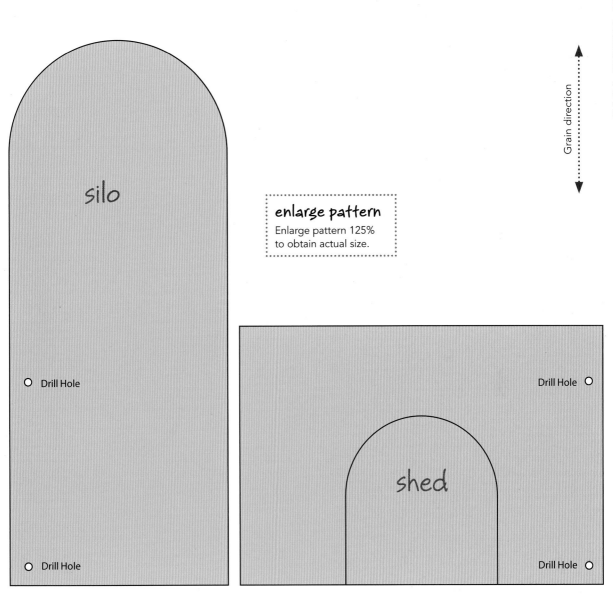

Grain direction

silo

enlarge pattern
Enlarge pattern 125%
to obtain actual size.

○ Drill Hole

○ Drill Hole

Drill Hole ○

shed

Drill Hole ○

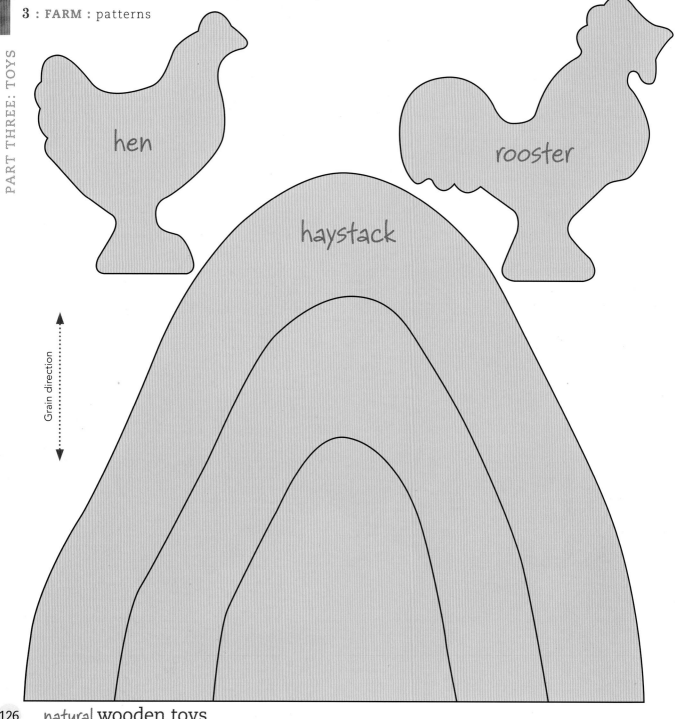

hen

rooster

haystack

Grain direction

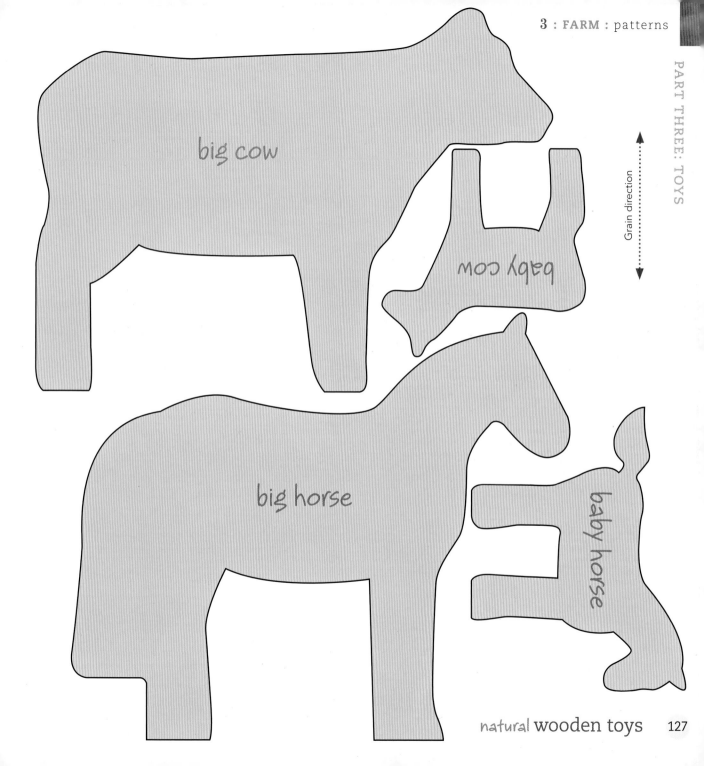

big cow

baby cow

Grain direction

big horse

baby horse

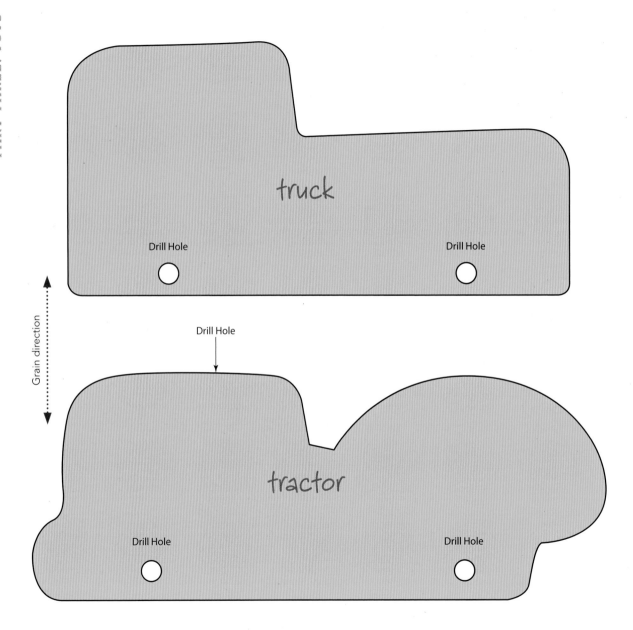

truck

Drill Hole

Drill Hole

Grain direction

Drill Hole

tractor

Drill Hole

Drill Hole

corn
stalks

butterfly wand

Drill Hole

mini
hay stack

hay bale

ladybug wand

Drill Hole

big pig

baby pig

Grain direction

natural wooden toys   129

4

ocean

The ocean is a magical place where imagination can come alive. The water is filled with waves and amazing creatures such as sea horses, dolphins, whales, turtles, colorful fish and, you never know, maybe a mermaid or two. Strike out on an adventure and sail your boat around a tropical island, where you discover erupting volcanoes. When your little ones come back on shore, they can explore the beach, play among the sand dunes and crabs, and even enjoy a magnificent sand castle.

nature walk

A walk along the beach at the ocean or wading into a stream can be an exciting adventure for the whole family. Children can discover the beauty of the beach and water while collecting items to include on their nature table and in their everyday play. Encouraging your children to collect smooth beach pebbles, shells, driftwood, dried seaweed, and other items during your nature walk helps to enrich their aquatic fantasies. Incorporating these beach and stream treasures into play helps children to remain in touch with the natural world around them.

sand castle

Spending the day building a sand castle is a wonderful way to enjoy the beach, but with this wooden sandcastle there is no need for your little ones to actually be at the beach. This castle is perfect for days when the weather is foul, or if you happen to be too far from a sandy beach. The fairytale castle found on page 78 can be easily transformed into the perfect sand castle with a little painting magic.

To transform the fairytale castle into the perfect sand castle, start by using a lovely sandy color of paint. We use a yellow base with a touch of brown added. Be sure to mix up plenty of paint so you do not run out before your castle is finished. To add some beach details, try painting seashells on the doorway and some seaweed around the base. Another approach to embellishing your castle would be to glue small seashells or bits of smooth sea glass to the castle.

turtles

Known to be slow and clumsy on land, these sea turtles glide through the water effortlessly with grace and speed. This mama and baby pair are sure to be favorites of your little one.

tools & materials

Wood, 3" x 6" x ¾" (75 x 150 x 20mm)

Non-toxic paint or dye, greens

Scroll saw or coping saw

Palm sander or 150-grit sandpaper and block

Paintbrush

Woodburner (optional)

Use the patterns on page 152.

mermaids

Your kids will fall in love with these beauties of the sea.

These mythological ladies are sure to facilitate hours

of ocean fantasy play. For a special surprise, give your

mermaid toy a paint job

that resembles your

little mermaid's hair

and eye color.

Use the patterns on page 156.

tools & materials

Wood, 4" x 6" x ¾" (100 x 150 x 20mm)

Non-toxic paint or dye, various colors

Scroll saw or coping saw

Palm sander or 150-grit sandpaper
    and block

Paintbrush

Woodburner (optional)

natural wooden toys   135

boat

No ocean would be complete without a seaworthy vessel. This little sailboat is the perfect little boat for your little one to sail in a creek, puddle, or the bathtub. If you plan on using your boat in water, it is best to leave the wood unpainted and apply two to four generous applications of beeswax before setting sail. If your boat enjoys quite a bit of time on the seas, make sure to reapply a bit of wood polish now and then to keep it watertight.

making the sail

I recommend using wool or craft felt for the sail. The advantage of using felt is that there are no raw edges to finish. Therefore, the mast can be easily sewn by hand in just a few minutes, even by a sewing novice. When you have cut out the sail, simply fold the left side over and put a simple seam across the top and down the side. Make sure there will be enough room for the dowel rod to fit.

tools & materials

Wood, 6" x 4" x ¾" (150 x 100 x 20mm)

Wood, 2½" x 1½" x ¼" (65 x 40 x 6mm)

Felt, 6" x 6" (150 x 150mm)

Dowel rod, 6" (150mm) long and ⅜" (10mm)-diameter

Wood glue

Scroll saw or coping saw

Palm sander or 150-grit sandpaper and block

Drill with ⅜" (10mm) bit

Use the patterns on page 157.

ADDITIONAL STEPS

Glue the smaller piece of wood on top of the main piece. After it has dried, drill a hole through the center of the small piece with a ⅜" (10mm) drill bit. Add a few drops of wood glue in the hole and insert the dowel rod. Apply 2–3 coats of wood polish, allowing polish to sit for an hour or so between waxings.

fish

These sweet little fish dart to and fro through a world of seaweed and coral. Your children will love painting these wooden clown and angelfish with all the tropical colors of the rainbow. Try using a woodburner to make any thin dark lines and to add other detail to your aquatic friends. Cut out several fish to make a whole school of fishy friends!

tools & materials

Wood, 3" x 6" x ¾" (75 x 150 x 20mm)

Non-toxic paint or dye, various colors

Scroll saw or coping saw

Palm sander or 150-grit sandpaper and block

Paintbrush

Woodburner (optional)

Use the patterns on page 153.

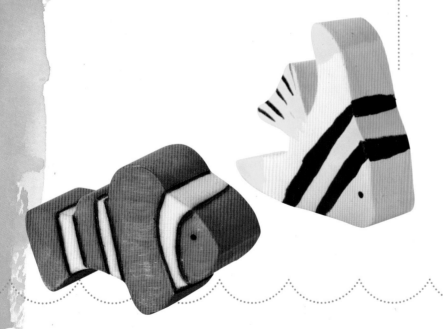

seahorse

Seahorses dart to and fro from their seaweed hiding places, zipping through dappled areas of sunshine and shade. It's no wonder children are fascinated by these tiny creatures, many of which are shaded so similarly to the foliage they twine their curly tails around. Of course, you don't have to keep the colors realistic! I've chosen a bright pink color for my version of this darling sea animal. The design also includes a base to hold the seahorse in upright position. I recommend cutting around the animal first, and then cutting out the base.

tools & materials

Wood, 3" x 6" x ¾" (75 x 150 x 20mm)

Non-toxic paint or dye, various colors

Scroll saw or coping saw

Palm sander or 150-grit sandpaper and block

Paintbrush

Woodburner (optional)

Use the patterns on page 157.

sand dune stacker

Sandy dunes are an important part of the beach. They not only protect the beaches from surging waves, but they also are a place for the small creatures of the beach to live. These wooden dunes will never wash away and are the perfect place for your children to hide their seashells and tuck away little wooden crabs and other beach beings.

tools & materials

Wood, 9" x 6" x ¾" (230 x 150 x 20mm)

Non-toxic paint or dye, yellow and brown

Scroll saw or coping saw

Palm sander or 150-grit sandpaper and block

Paintbrush

Use the patterns on page 155.

PAINTING TIPS

A mixture of yellow and brown paint is perfect for the different pieces of the sand dune stacker. The smallest pieces can be painted the darkest shade of tan, with each successive piece a slightly lighter shade of golden brown.

crabs

These happy little crabs will soon have your little ones

scuttling crab-style around the house. I recommend

using a woodburner to detail this design—the darkness

really pops against the bright warm colors that look

fitting on a crab.

tools & materials

Wood, 3" x 6" x ¾" (75 x 150 x 20mm)

Non-toxic paint or dye, red and orange

Scroll saw or coping saw

Palm sander or 150-grit sandpaper
  and block

Paintbrush

Woodburner (optional)

Use the patterns on page 153.

seaweed and mini wave

Try making some fun accessories to enhance the beach time fun! These miniature waves and seaweed will give the creatures of the sea a place to hide and play.

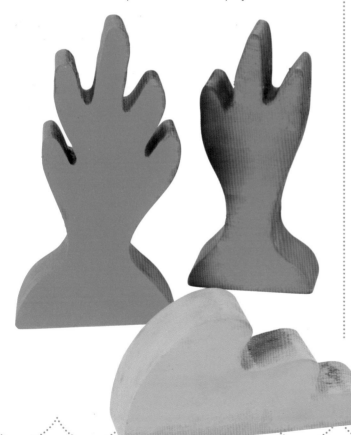

tools & materials

Wood, 3½" x 6" x ¾" (90 x 150 x 20mm)

Non-toxic paint or dye, greens and blues

Scroll saw or coping saw

Palm sander or 150-grit sandpaper and block

Paintbrush

Use the patterns on page 153.

wave stacker

No beach is complete without waves. Some of those waves gently lap at the beach, creating tide pools that abound with magical sea creatures, but other waves surge forward, carrying surfboarders and crashing ashore. The wooden wave stacker is three waves in one, so there is sure to be the perfect wave for every occasion.

tools & materials

Wood, 6" x 5" x ¾" (150 x 127 x 20mm)

Non-toxic paint or dye, blue and white

Scroll saw or coping saw

Palm sander or 150-grit sandpaper and block

Paintbrush

Use the patterns on page 157.

PAINTING TIPS

Mixtures of blue and white paints are perfect for the different pieces of the wave stacker. I suggest making the smallest piece of the wave the darkest shade of blue. Then, for each sequential piece, just add a bit more white to the blue paint to make lighter shades of blue.

whales

These friendly whales come with a removable spout for an extra splash of fun. Your child will have a blast playing with these—you might even get them to remember that whales are the largest animals alive on the planet but feed on tiny little things like krill and plankton! Who wouldn't be impressed by that?

tools & materials

Wood, 8" x 6" x ¾" (205 x 150 x 20mm)

Dowel

Non-toxic paint or dye, various colors

Scroll saw or coping saw

Palm sander or 150-grit sandpaper and block

Paintbrush

Woodburner (optional)

Use the patterns on page 154.

PAINTING TIPS

For a realistic painting effect as seen here, it is best to start with the lightest color and gradually work your way darker. Thin the paint a bit to help blend the colors. If you are in doubt, try blending on a few scraps of wood and within no time you will be a painting pro.

volcano stacker

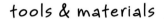

Many tropical islands are home to active volcanoes. Volcanoes are so intriguing to children—lava and explosions, how thrilling! You can make your own wooden volcano for your children to enjoy that's not nearly so dangerous, but just as exciting. The wooden volcano stacker can be inactive, but when your little ones are ready for some excitement, just add the lava piece for an instant eruption.

tools & materials

Wood, 6" x 5" x ¾" (150 x 127 x 20mm)

Non-toxic paint or dye, gray, brown, orange, and red

Scroll saw or coping saw

Palm sander or 150-grit sandpaper and block

Paintbrush

Use the patterns on page 152.

PAINTING TIPS

I suggest painting the volcano body pieces a mixture of gray and brown. The smallest piece is primarily brown, with just a touch of gray. For each sequential piece, add a bit more gray to the paint to create a lighter color. A mixture of red and orange is ideal to give a true-to-life lava shade.

dolphins

This chipper dolphin pair is only too glad to do flips and tricks for your kids. Try cutting out a hoop for the dolphins to jump through, or scroll a big red ball for them to push around. The fun wave base will keep the big dolphin in a cool leaping pose—and also serves as a simple puzzle. I recommend cutting around the dolphin first, and then cutting out the base.

tools & materials

Wood, 5" x 6" x ¾" (128 x 150 x 20mm)

Non-toxic paint or dye, gray, white, and blue

Scroll saw or coping saw

Palm sander or 150-grit sandpaper and block

Paintbrush

Woodburner (optional)

Use the patterns on page 156.

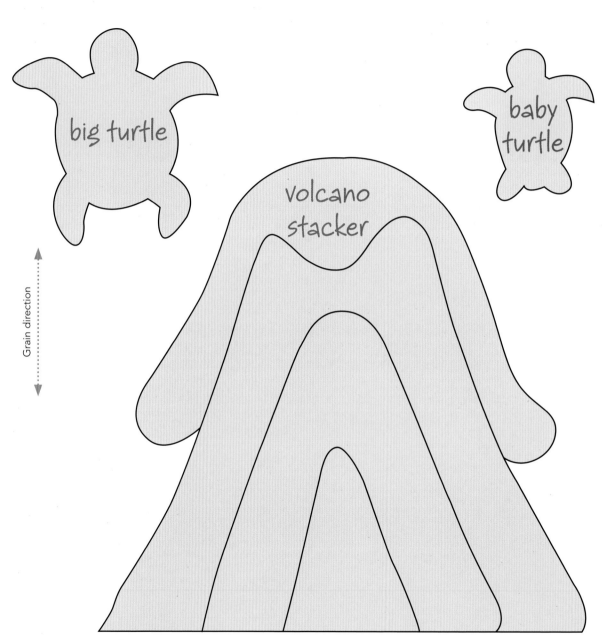

big turtle

baby turtle

volcano stacker

Grain direction

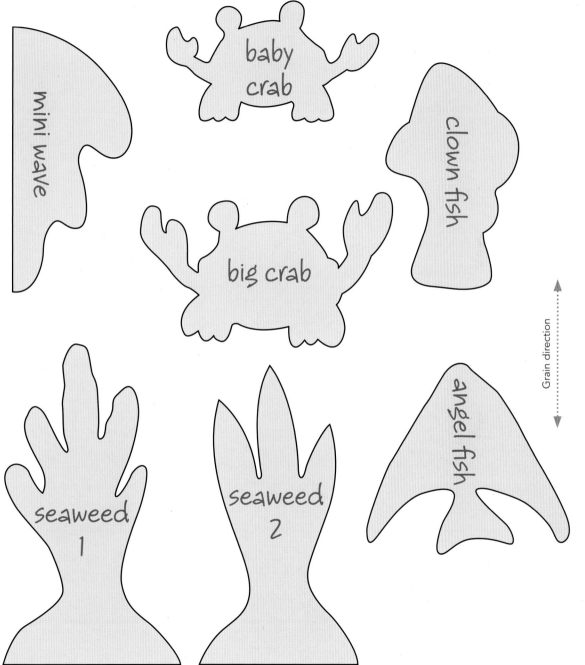

mini wave

baby crab

clown fish

big crab

Grain direction

angel fish

seaweed 1

seaweed 2

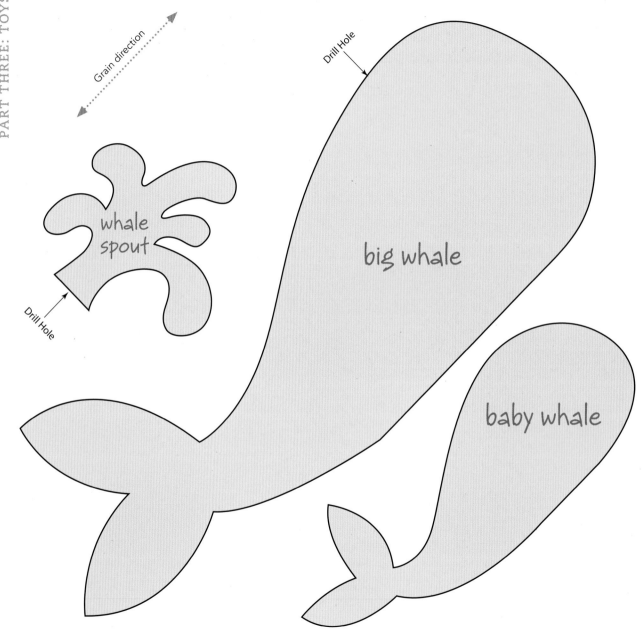

Grain direction

Drill Hole

whale spout

Drill Hole

big whale

baby whale

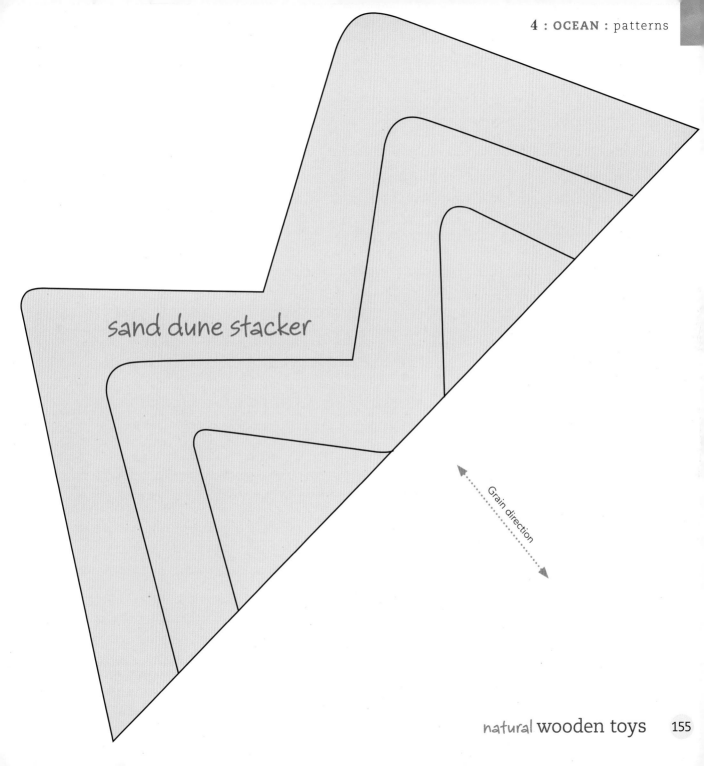

sand dune stacker

Grain direction

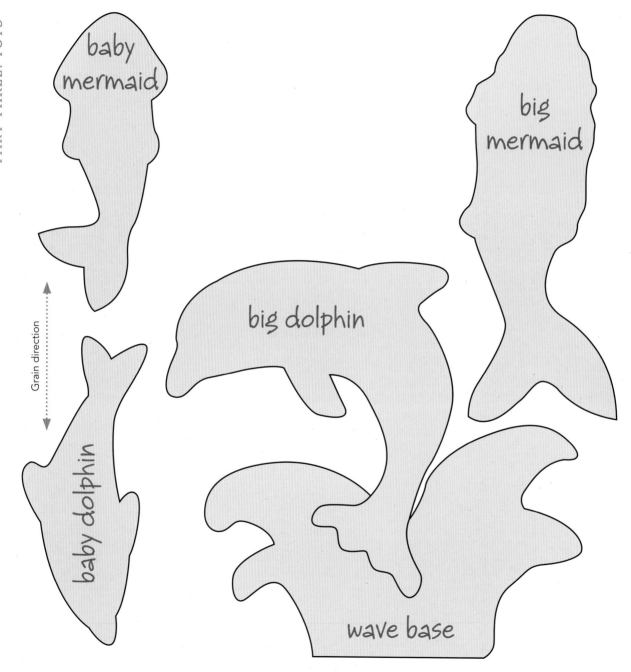

baby
mermaid

big
mermaid

Grain direction

big dolphin

baby dolphin

wave base

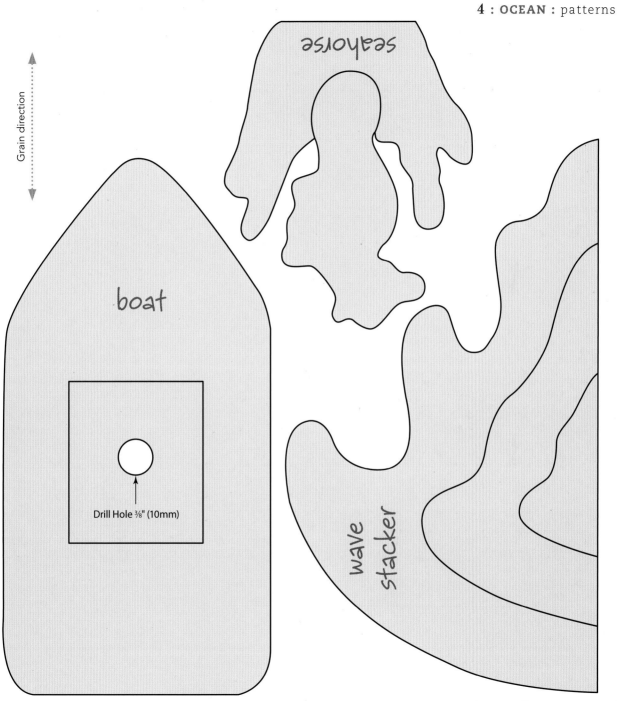

Grain direction

seahorse

boat

Drill Hole ⅜" (10mm)

wave stacker

5

city

The city is a hustling and bustling place with tall buildings that tower above the streets, where cars whiz by and taxis honk their horns. In the sky, helicopters dart here and there, while airplanes soar high above. Trains filled with busy travelers snake through tunnels underground. Amidst all the noise, some peace and quiet can be found at the city park, where water fountains bubble and shady trees grow.

cityscape stacker

The trademark of most large cities is their unique skyline.

This stacker is sure to be your city's very own trademark.

Make one or many and paint them in different ways to

bring your town to life. Add extra windows if you like.

If your child has a favorite city, try

adapting the design to reflect

its cityscape.

tools & materials

Wood, 10" x 6" x ¾" (255 x 150 x 20mm)

Non-toxic paint or dye, gray, black, and blue

Scroll saw or coping saw

Palm sander or 150-grit sandpaper and block

Paintbrush

Use the patterns on page 174.

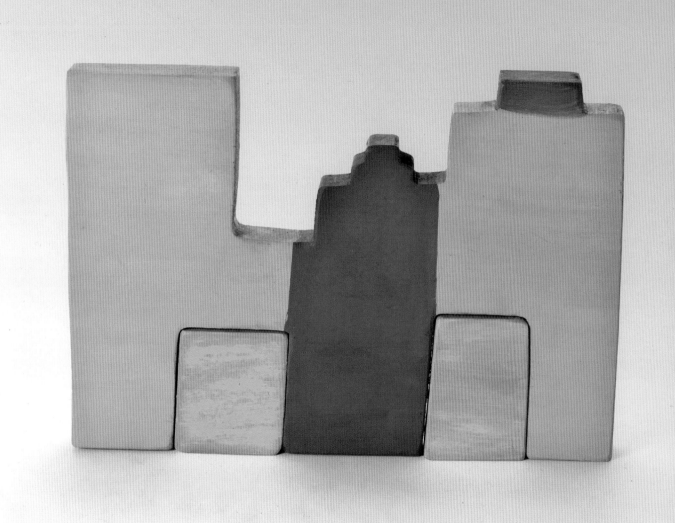

car

Have somewhere to be? Use this car to get there quickly!

This sedan is perfect for the streets of the big city, but if

you'd rather not park your own car, you can easily paint it

as a cab.

taxi cab

It is easy to transform your unpainted sedan into a taxi cab. Mix some yellow paint with a touch of orange to make that famous taxi cab yellow color. Use black paint and a fine paintbrush to add the details such as the word "Taxi," or even checkers if you are feeling really creative and patient.

police cruiser

For a police car, simply divide the car in thirds—paint the middle third white and the outer two thirds a dark blue. In the white portion, you could add a yellow star or another law enforcement symbol. If you would like to add a siren, simply drill a hole on the top of the car, paint the top of a dowel red, and glue in place.

tools & materials

Wood, 4" x 6" x ¾" (100 x 150 x 20mm)

Non-toxic paint or dye, various colors

Scroll saw or coping saw

Palm sander or 150-grit sandpaper and block

Drill with ⁷⁄₃₂" (5.5mm) bit

Paintbrush

Store-bought wooden wheels per vehicle, 1½" (38mm) diameter, ½" (13mm) thick, 4

Wooden pegs to serve as axles per vehicle, 1¼" (32mm) long, ⁷⁄₃₂" (5.5mm) thick, 4

Wood glue

Mallet or hammer

Use the patterns on page 175.

ADDITIONAL STEPS

Use the drill where shown on the pattern to create the holes for the wheel axles. Install the axles and wheels with a little wood glue, and use a mallet to tap them home. You might need to snip off the ends of the axles if they are too long.

helicopter

If you are really in a hurry, take a ride in the helicopter to get there fast. Your little one will have a blast rolling their helicopter around and then taking to the skies with a propeller that really goes. Just imagine the amazing view from up there!

ADDITIONAL STEPS

Use the drill where shown on the pattern to create the holes for the wheel axles and the propeller on the top of the helicopter. Install the axles, wheels, and propeller with a little wood glue. Be careful to not use too much glue, because excess glue may seep up through the holes and onto the helicopter body. If this happens, the wheels may get glued in place. You might need to tap the axles into place with a hammer or mallet. Take care when placing the axles for the wheels and propeller—make sure not to tap the axle in too much, therefore making the fit too tight. If this happens, the wheels and propeller will not spin well.

tools & materials

Wood, 6" x 6" x ¾" (150 x 150 x 20mm)

Non-toxic paint or dye, various colors

Scroll saw or coping saw

Palm sander or 150-grit sandpaper and block

Drill with ⁷⁄₃₂" (5.5mm) bit

Paintbrush

4 Store-bought wooden wheels per vehicle, 1¼" (32mm) diameter, ⁷⁄₁₆" (11mm) thick

5 Wooden pegs to serve as axles per vehicle, 1¼" (32mm) long, ⁷⁄₃₂" (5.5mm) thick

Wood glue

Mallet or hammer

Use the patterns on page 176.

airplane

Get ready to soar near and far with your own airplane, complete with wheels that roll and a propeller that spins. This airplane doesn't need its own airport, just some imagination and a bit of kid power to take it up into the big blue skies.

ADDITIONAL STEPS

Use the drill where shown on the pattern to create the holes for the wheel axles and propeller. Install the axles, wheels, and propeller with a little wood glue. Be careful to not use too much glue, because excess glue may seep up through the holes and onto the body. If this happens, the wheels may get glued in place. You might need to tap the axles into place with a hammer or mallet. Take care when placing the axles—make sure not to tap the axle in too much, therefore making the fit too tight. If this happens, the wheels and propeller will not spin well.

To affix the airplane's wing, first drill two holes in the center of the wing. Then place the wing on the plane with the holes aligned on the top of the airplane. Use a pen to make a mark where each hole is located. Now you have the proper placement for drilling holes in the plane body. Drill those holes. Next, add a bit of wood glue to each hole, place the pegs through the wing holes, and gently tap into place. Make sure the wing is snug to the body of the plane.

tools & materials

Wood for body, 8" x 6" x ¾" (205 x 150 x 20mm)

Wood for wing, 7¼" x 1½" x ¼" (185 x 40 x 6mm)

Wood for propeller, 2½" x 1" x ¼" (65 x 25 x 6mm)

Non-toxic paint or dye, various colors

Scroll saw or coping saw

Palm sander or 150-grit sandpaper and block

Drill with ⁷⁄₃₂" (5.5mm) bit

Paintbrush

2 Store-bought wooden wheels per vehicle, 1½" (38mm) diameter, ½" (13mm) thick

5 Wooden pegs to serve as axles per vehicle, 1¼" (32mm) long, ⁷⁄₃₂" (5.5mm) thick

Wood glue

Mallet or hammer

Use the patterns on page 177.

fountain stacker

One of the highlights of taking a stroll through a city park is the beautiful fountains that you encounter. Add a bit of beauty and fun to your city park by making a fountain stacker. The pretend inhabitants of your city can sit by it, feed the pigeons, and throw in pennies.

tools & materials

Wood, 8" x 6" x ¾" (205 x 150 x 20mm)

Dowel rod, 1" x ⅝" (25 x 16mm) diameter

Non-toxic paint or dye, various colors

Scroll saw or coping saw

Palm sander or 150-grit sandpaper and block

Drill with ⅝" (16mm) bit

Paintbrush

Mallet or hammer

Use the patterns on page 178.

ADDITIONAL STEPS

To affix the dowel to the base of your fountain, drill a hole in the middle of the base. Add a drop or two of wood glue to the hole and gently press the dowel piece into place. If the fit is really tight, just use a mallet or hammer to tap it into place. This dowel will fit into the largest piece of the fountain water. Drill a hole at the bottom of this piece. Make this hole a slight bit bigger by gently pressing the sides of the hole into the drill bit. This will allow for easy on and off of the water pieces. If you would like the fountain to be permanently affixed, just add a bit of wood glue to the water piece, place it on the dowel rod, and allow to dry.

park trees

The park is a place to go to get away from the busy pace of the big city and enjoy nature. Trees are instrumental to getting back to nature in a park. They block out the sights and sounds that can be so overwhelming in the city. These trees are the perfect addition for your city park. The rocks at the base of the trees add a bit more stability and style to your trees.

tools & materials

Wood, 8" x 6" x ¾" (205 x 150 x 20mm)

Wood, 4" x 1½" x ¼" (100 x 40 x 6mm)

Non-toxic paint or dye, gray, brown, and green

Scroll saw or coping saw

Palm sander or 150-grit sandpaper and block

Paintbrush

Wood glue

Use the patterns on pages 179 and 180.

ADDITIONAL STEPS

Apply a small amount of wood glue to the rocks and place them on the base of the tree. Make sure the rocks are even with the bottom of the tree.

train

Choo, choo! Hop on the train to Imagination Town. This little train is perfect for your little one who loves things that go! If you would like a long train, try making a few extra middle cars and painting them all in a different way.

ADDITIONAL STEPS

Drill holes in the train cars, where shown, for wheels.

Round the edges of the connector pieces on each car. The easiest way to do this is to aggressively sand the outer edges of the connector pieces with a rough grade of sand paper. This will allow the hinging to move freely. When the connector pieces are sanded, drill a hole all the way through them. There are two types of connector pieces. The higher ones will have a peg (the same axles as used for the wheels) permanently affixed. Drill the holes on the top connectors the same size as the axle. When drilling the holes in the bottom connectors, use a drill bit the next size up so the peg can be easily removed. Next, gently tap pegs into the top connectors. The bottom part of the peg should go all the way through the connector and have a bit of excess hanging down. This excess is the part that will fit into the lower connector holes.

To add the wheels, put a few drips of glue into the holes. Assemble each axle and wheel set and gently tap the axles into the holes.

tools & materials

Wood, 15" x 4" x ¾" (380 x 100 x 20mm)

Non-toxic paint or dye, various colors

Scroll saw or coping saw

Palm sander or 150-grit sandpaper and block

Drill with ⁷⁄₃₂" (5.5mm) bit

Paintbrush

Mallet or hammer

Wooden wheels for a 3-piece train, 1½" (38mm) diameter, ½" (13mm) thick, 12

Wooden peg axles for a 3-piece train, 1¼" (32mm) long, ⁷⁄₃₂" (5.5mm) diameter, 14

Wood glue

Use the patterns on pages 181 and 182.

Grain direction

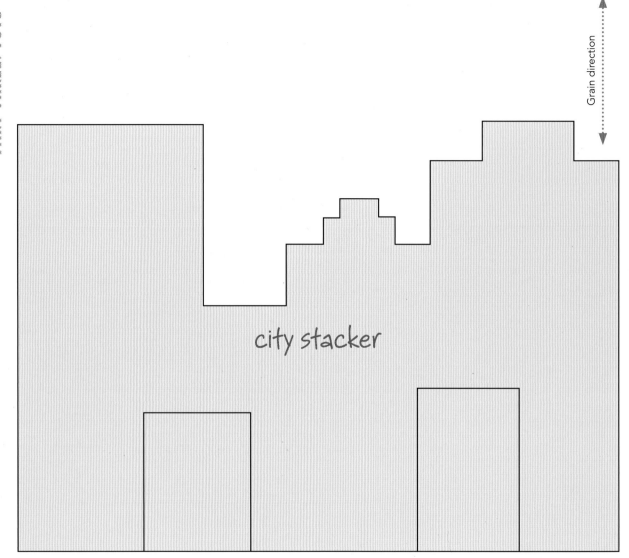

city stacker

enlarge pattern
Enlarge pattern 125%
to obtain actual size.

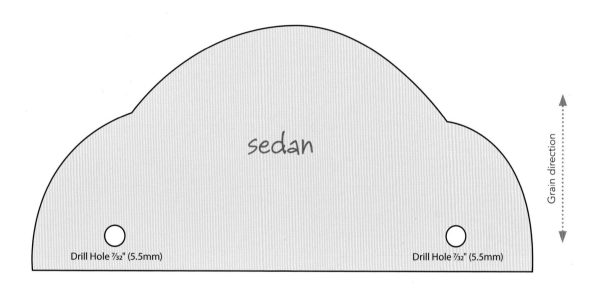

sedan

Grain direction

Drill Hole 7/32" (5.5mm)

Drill Hole 7/32" (5.5mm)

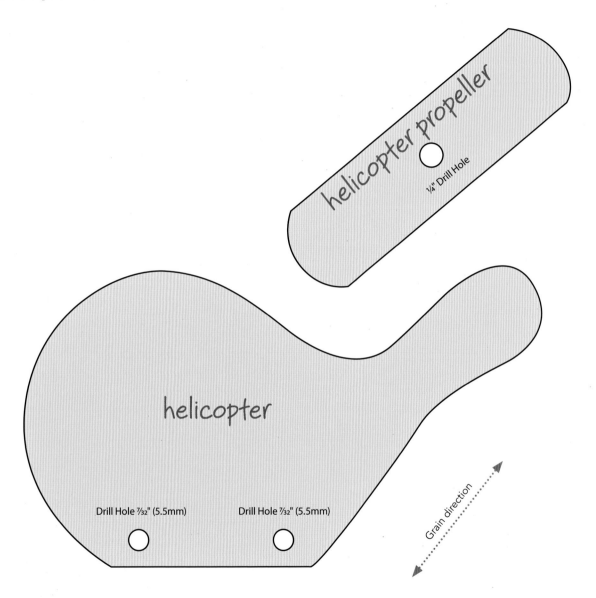

helicopter propeller

¼" Drill Hole

helicopter

Drill Hole ⁷⁄₃₂" (5.5mm)   Drill Hole ⁷⁄₃₂" (5.5mm)

Grain direction

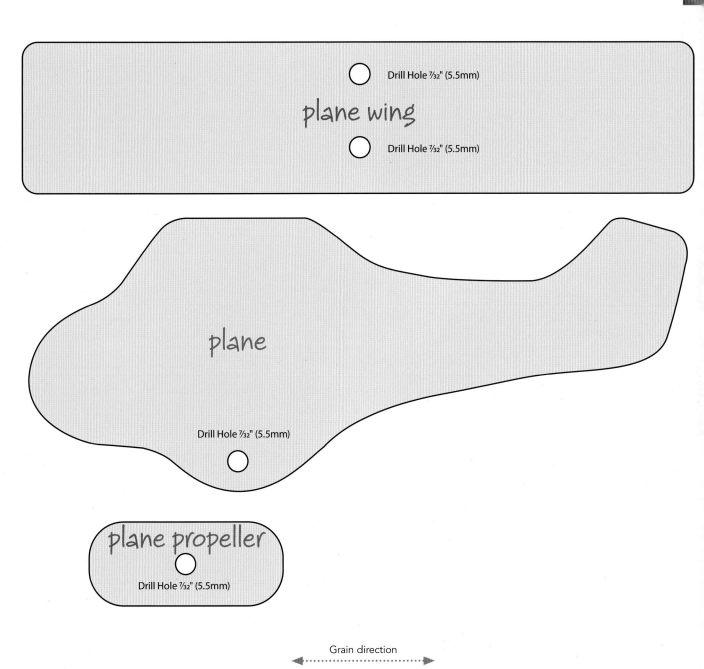

Drill Hole ⁷⁄₃₂" (5.5mm)

plane wing

Drill Hole ⁷⁄₃₂" (5.5mm)

plane

Drill Hole ⁷⁄₃₂" (5.5mm)

plane propeller

Drill Hole ⁷⁄₃₂" (5.5mm)

Grain direction

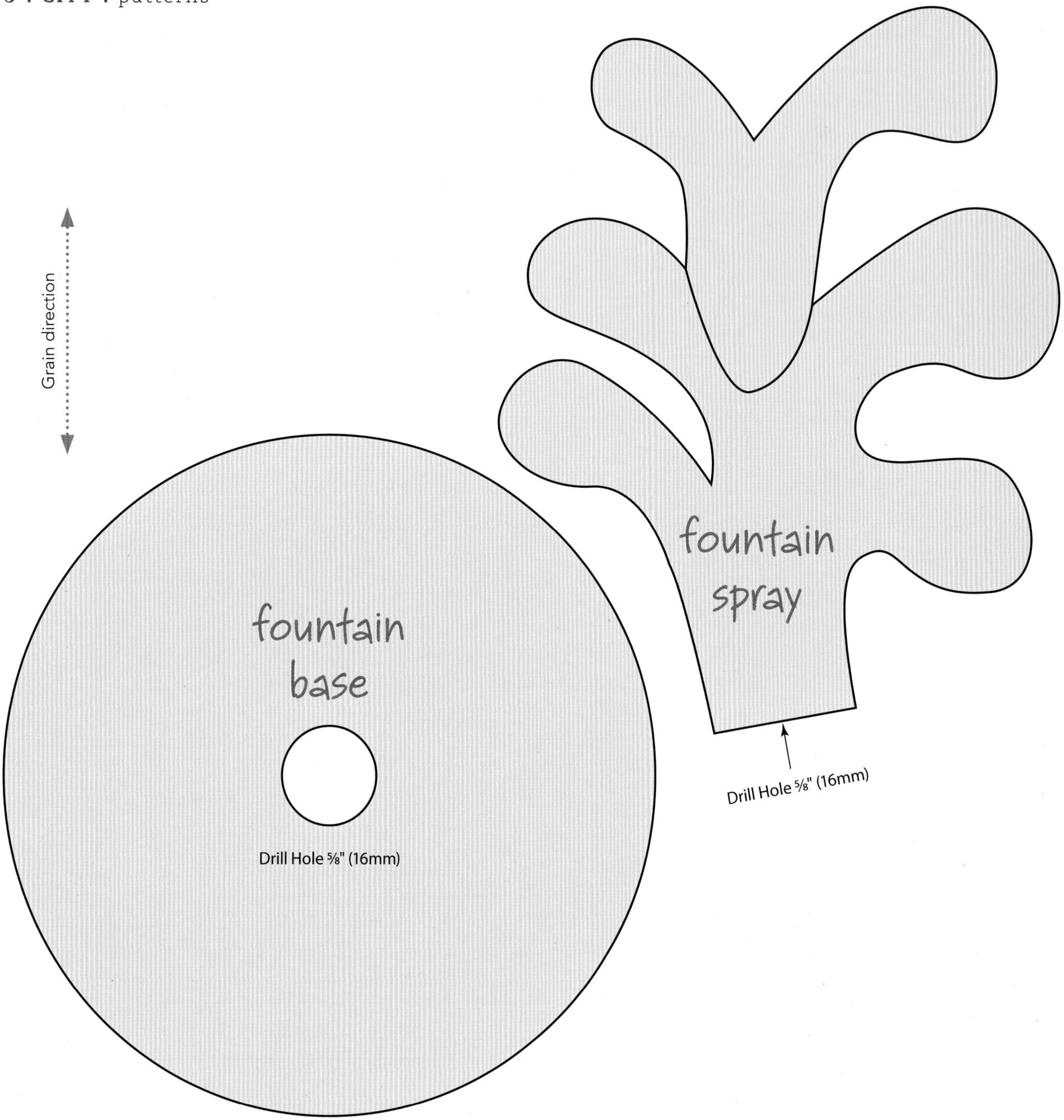

Grain direction

fountain
spray

Drill Hole ⅝" (16mm)

fountain
base

Drill Hole ⅝" (16mm)

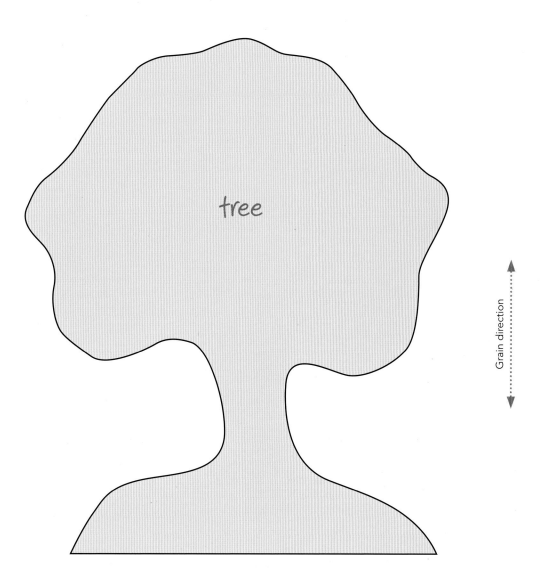

tree

Grain direction

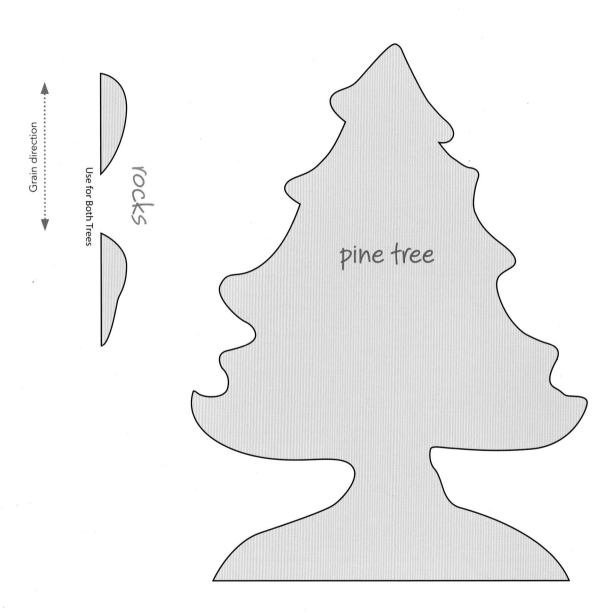

Grain direction

Use for Both Trees

rocks

pine tree

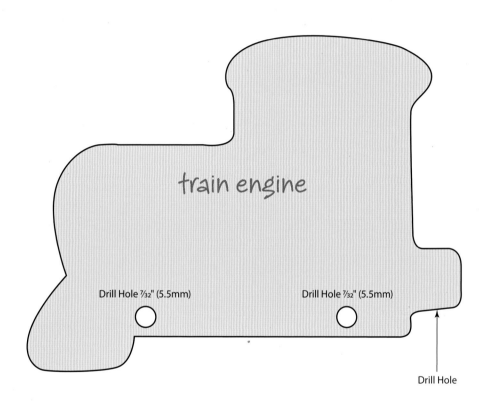

train engine

Drill Hole 7/32" (5.5mm)

Drill Hole 7/32" (5.5mm)

Drill Hole

Grain direction

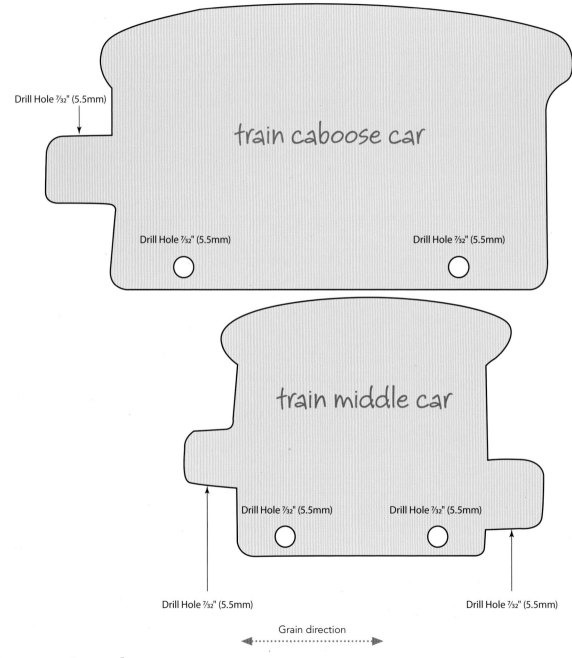

Drill Hole 7/32" (5.5mm)

train caboose car

Drill Hole 7/32" (5.5mm)

Drill Hole 7/32" (5.5mm)

train middle car

Drill Hole 7/32" (5.5mm)

Drill Hole 7/32" (5.5mm)

Drill Hole 7/32" (5.5mm)

Drill Hole 7/32" (5.5mm)

Grain direction

natural **wooden toys**

index

acquisition & book editor
Kerri Landis

copy editors
Paul Hambke & Heather Stauffer

cover & layout designer
Lindsay Hess

cover & project photographer
Scott Kriner

proofreader
Lynda Jo Runkle

indexer
Jay Kreider

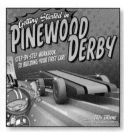
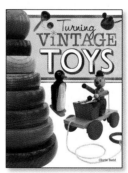